'Have You Got... (The Ejected Story)

By

Jim Brooks

Chapter One

It was the arse end of February 2020 and I was stood centre stage in a hot and sweaty club in Florida with a microphone in one hand and a cold can of Guinness in the other. I was staring out at the crowd of about two hundred assorted young and old punks and skins all slam dancing, wrecking, stage diving, shouting, cheering and singing along to a song that I wrote almost forty years ago.

It was just before the Covid pandemic had broken out and The Ejected were headlining We Are The Punx 3 festival at Respectable Street club, West Palm Beach, South Florida.

I was dripping in sweat, breathing hard and a bit pissed but loving every second of it as the boys in the band blasted out around me and the stage lights shone in my face. I looked out at a sea of colourful punk rock faces, who were all staring up at us, totally loving this old punk and Oi band.

Certainly a far cry from the early days of being in The Ejected I can tell you.

At the grand old age of 61, you could say that I was finally and ironically living out the ultimate 'teenage' dream.

Definitely a dream that the spotty, naive and shy teenage Jim Brooks back in the late 1970's had been fantasising about, as he sat, strumming on his cheap acoustic guitar in the front bedroom of his parent's house in Marston Avenue, Dagenham, Essex all those years ago.

Now, forty-five years later, I was stood on stage, some four and a half thousand miles away from home, I was feeling almost like a superstar. Well a superstar for one night anyway maybe, ha ha.

I remember thinking it seemed so surreal that I was the reason that all these American fans had travelled here from around the country to come just to see The Ejected play a live show.

During the evening, whilst other acts were belting out their sets up on stage, I wandered around inside and outside the club chatting, smoking, drinking and laughing with so many fans. I shook hands, posed for selfies and signed my autograph when asked. I listened to them telling me how much The Ejected and our songs had meant to them. It never stops amazing me that the songs I have written could mean so much to other people, especially halfway around the world. I know saying that might make me sound a bit 'wanky' or 'precious' but it's honestly the truth. I suppose I'd never really expected the Ejected songs and records to have travelled so far and wide or to have been enjoyed so much by people in other countries.

Since reforming The Ejected back in 2014 I have been genuinely surprised and sometimes overwhelmed by the amount of loyalty and love the fans seem to have for the band. If only I had realised how much we had been missed over the years since we split back in 1984, then I'd have definitely reformed The Ejected a lot sooner.

I was born in Bromley in Kent and after my parents moved around a bit, when I was a baby, we finally ended up in a ground floor flat on a council estate in South London, at the bottom of Beckenham Hill Road where it meets Downham Way, not too far from Catford, Lewisham and Grove Park. So from the age of about five up until ten I grew up south of the river. My dad was working at Fords in Dagenham at this time (the other side of the Blackwall Tunnel) and it was a bit of a trek for him travelling sixteen miles to work and back every day, using only public transport. Especially as he worked three different weekly, shift patterns (earlies, lates and nights) in weekly rotation, so obviously my parents were looking for a council exchange to somewhere in Dagenham, so he could be nearer to his job. It was a thing you could do back then, agree a swap with a council tenant from any of the other London boroughs who were looking to be closer to work, family or friends and sort it out between the two councils, no problem.

Anyway my parents found an old lady who was rattling around in a big semi-detached house in Dagenham and missing all her old pals in south London, so in 1968 we swapped our ground floor, two bedroomed flat in Flower House Estate, London SE6 for her three-bedroomed house in Dagenham.

I was ten years old at the time and about to start my final year in junior school, so it was a bit of a wrench for me having to leave all of my little mates behind on the council estate and at my old school, to start afresh in an area that I knew fuck all about.

Moving to Dagenham at that time was a bit of a shock for me I can tell you. I was like a fish out of water. All the kids at school were asking me what football team I supported and when I told them Manchester United it did not go down very well at all.

I had not really followed football that much up until then, apart from watching Manchester United beat Benfica, live on the telly in the '1967-68' European Cup final at Wembley. That's how come I had started to support them.

In fact, I only have vague memories of England beating West Germany in the '66 World cup final as I was only 8 years old at the time. I remember that we had gone over to my Uncle Teddy's house in Gillingham to watch the final on his brand new television with some of our other relatives. But I was too busy playing out in the back garden with all my young cousins to really take too much interest in the game. I can vaguely remember my dad shouting out for me to come inside to watch and witness this momentous and significant event in English football history, as it was such a rarity. I'd just watch a few minutes then tear off back outside to play with my young cousins again and was only aware of the game whenever I heard a loud groan or cheer from everyone inside the house watching the game that would make me go back inside to ask "What's happening?"

For fucks sake!

How I wish I had listened to my old man and sat down to watch England's glorious victory that day. Little did I realise, at the time, how fucking rare it would be for the England football team to win anything else again in like fucking forever in the decades to come.

Grrrrr!

Anyway where was I?

Oh yeah, Dagenham.

"You should support West ham mate," my new school chums had aggressively advised me, "Cos they're in the First Division and are the local team," (7 miles away in fact) "or support Dagenham FC, who are in the Isthmian league." The 'Daggers' were even closer apparently (literally three streets away from my new family home). So I had felt more than a bit threatened already, for just liking the wrong fucking football team. Then at my new school, Five Elms Juniors, when we had PE which consisted of an hour a week playing a game of football over the local playing fields I only had a cheap green football shirt with white collar and cuffs to wear. This had been fine back at my old south London school, where First Division football hadn't been much of a thing apparently. Probably because the only local clubs to us on that council estate had been Crystal Palace, Charlton and Millwall.

Anyway all my new school mates had pointed at me laughing and jeering and asking me why was I wearing a Northern Ireland football shirt? I also had on a pair of cheap, nasty football boots that my mum had bought me from Woolworths, which seemed to amuse them all greatly.

So it wasn't the best of starts is all I am saying.

I was an outsider in those Dagenham kids' eyes and a bit of a twat too. It wasn't my fault that my parent's now had four kids to clothe and feed and a big house to pay bills for with only my dad working. So I suppose school PE kit and football boots were quite low down on my mum's list of priorities back then.

By the way I hope I'm not boring you so far, by banging on about all this 'poor little Jim Brooks growing up' stuff?

When I decided to write this book I didn't know where to start really. In most autobiographies and biographies of bands and musicians that I've read, they all seem to start at the beginning, which is logical I suppose, but with some in my opinion it can go on a bit too long and can get a bit boring. In the few decent ones I've read the early years stuff can explain a lot and be hilarious, sad, traumatic, scary but also very illuminating too. It all depends on how entertaining the author is or how truthful and real those memories really are?

Anyway I'm trying to give you an honest account of how I managed to form a punk band back then but also giving you a bit of the 'gritty early years stuff' without going on too much. I don't want you all to be rolling your eyes or yawning and muttering 'Come on you prick, get on with it' in the first chapter do I? I have also just realised that if you are reading this book, then you've probably already shelled out the cash to buy it, so I could if I wasn't bothered about it so much I suppose just roll out a basic band history, members and discography thing couldn't I?

As you've already bought it.

So please bear with me for a bit longer while I explain what those early years were like for me and I'll try and keep it as entertaining as possible for you.

So onto big school, which turned out to be Parsloes Manor Comprehensive, in the next year when I had just turned eleven.

Back then in your final year of junior school, you did an exam called The Eleven Plus and it determined your level of education and to what type of school you were allocated a spot at, either a grammar school for the smart pupils or the local comprehensive for the rest. I actually passed that Eleven Plus exam and was one of only five pupils out of the whole year of Five Elms junior school to pass it.

But here's a life changing moment: there were only four places up for grabs at Dagenham County High Grammar School from Five Elms Junior school. So guess who was the one out of five to miss out on a place?

As the headmaster later explained to my mystified and rather annoyed parents, that I had missed out on a grammar school place because I'd only joined Five Elms school for the final year, after moving from south London, (not my fault) and the other four boys had been at the school from the start and so it was decided (on that reason alone) that I would not get my well-deserved chance to go to the then prestigious Dagenham County High Grammar school as a student.

Instead, I was to be lumped in with the 'oi polloi' and 'plebs' at the local comprehensive, as my mother had rather cynically remarked at the time.

So fate had steered the young Jim Brooks away from academic greatness and superior learning and obviously had a totally different plan for him.

So big school loomed and I didn't fair very well. I was a shy and quite naïve kid plus I was new to the area and not familiar with all the mean streets of Barking and Dagenham.

I had only a handful of friends and hated being at school. I wasn't a troublemaker or a joker, nor did I play truant much. I obeyed all the rules and attended all lessons on the timetable and was generally a very well behaved student. I tried my best at every subject and was mostly above average intellectually. My best subjects were Art, Maths and Physics. I loved English but the teachers advised my parents against letting me taking it at 'O' level exam standard. I was advised to take CSE's instead and told that I would need to stay on as a sixth former if I wanted to take 'O' levels in any of those subjects. Except for English as they didn't think I could pass it. Bastards! (Now look at me with all my self-published novels up on Amazon Kindle).

I also suffered a couple of years (2nd and 3rd year mostly) from persistent bullying in school. I have no idea why they used to pick on me so much, I suppose it was because I looked like a victim maybe. I was pushed off a high wall by one of them outside the Imperial War Museum on a school trip. And on a Geography field trip the bullies cornered me behind the coach and dared one of them to punch me in the face, which he did and they all laughed and walked away. Cunts! I went home with a black eye but none of the teachers seemed bothered. In fact the teachers at that school were mostly pricks too. I did not really have the courage to tell any of them that having my dinner money nicked, sweets confiscated and school books knocked out of my hands was happening on a daily basis. Being a 'grass' was apparently the worst thing you could be labelled back then.

Different times eh?

I tolerated it all for a year and a half until one day I decided I'd had enough.

It all came to a head, when I was so pissed off with nobody seemingly bothered or interested in helping me that one day I just refused to go to school.

I had finally had enough.

My parents asked me why and I told them everything.

I remember the headmaster of the school coming round our house to speak to me and my parents later that day. He seemed especially concerned as to why I was suddenly and steadfastly refusing to go to school.

So I told him very bluntly about everything that was happening to me in his school, right under his fucking nose. I named names and told him that I was never going back there.

The headmaster Mr Grainger sat drinking tea with me and my parents (like it was all some bizarre dream) as I told them all about the five or six nasty students who had been continually picking on me, nicking my dinner money, my sweets or generally punching and spitting at me or calling me nasty names for the best part of two years. I named the culprits too (who were Frank Konchesky, Tony Carter, Ian Hater, Michael Kettlety, Richard Woodward and Geoff Birch) like a 'Supergrass' ha ha, and later that day all six were instantly suspended from school for a week and their parents reprimanded. They were all told not to go near me again (in or out of school) or they would face getting instantly expelled.

So I was coaxed into going back to school and for a time things did improve.

Even after the six bullying cunts did return they would still occasionally verbally threaten me or spit in my face (like the cowardly bullying pricks they were) but always out of the sight of any potential witnesses.

I sometimes wish that I could have bumped into any of them in the decades that followed because after I left school I gained more confidence, got physically stronger and certainly a lot surer of myself and I quite fancied the thought of chinning one or all of them in revenge, or the idea of giving each a good kicking in vengeful retribution. It never happened though.

If my life was a Hollywood movie then maybe I could have hunted all six of the cunts down and tortured them to a bloody death in revenge but sadly, real life is just not like that is it?

There was a bully at junior school called Clifford Mathews though who everyone was scared of at the time. Then about five years later I was playing footy with my mates over the local playing field and I spotted 'bully boy' Mathews walking past us down a public footpath fenced off that ran alongside of the field and he was staring through the six foot high, wire fence at us aggressively. So, I went right over, asking him through the wire fence, something like, 'Who the fuck are you looking at?' He squared up to me and said 'Come on then," or something like that and so I felt a sudden rush of anger rise up inside me (probably from all those previous years of being bullied) and I started climbing the fence to get over and lamp him one. To my absolute surprise by the time I had reached the top of the fence the cunt was running away as fast as he could. Like the cowardly fucker he obviously was and I felt a great swell of pride and self-worth in my chest, especially as all my footy mates were watching and cheering me on.

I remember something changing in me that day.

To this day I can't tolerate or watch bullying, of the verbal or aggressive kind by anybody, as it always riles and stirs me up and I have always interjected whenever possible to administer a warning or a slap.

So school was a mixed bag for the 'young me' and I had to stay on an extra year in the sixth form to try and pass four 'O' level exams, which I did pass first time (Hurrah) in Art, Physics, Maths and Technical Drawing.

At job interviews and on my CV I always list 5 'O' levels, adding English, as I still think that I'd have passed the exam if I'd been allowed to take it.

So as school was not a place that I made many friends in good old Dagenham, I mostly relied on the kids that lived down my road to be my mates during my early teens. My only interests in those early teen years were television shows, comic books, football, sci-fi books and music.

Growing up in front of the television and radio in the 60's and 70's was the best. I often think that I am so lucky to have lived through those two explosive decades which were growing and thriving in so many entertainment areas. Comedy shows, Dramas, Cop shows, cartoons, American telly shows, pop music shows and such.

Kids Comics were prolific back then too and I loved comics so much in my early years. We had the Beezer, Beano, Dandy, Topper, Whizzer n Chips, Buster, Cor, Sparky and many others. Also Marvel and DC superhero comics were becoming available and so I would often spunk all of my weekly pocket money away on Spiderman, the Incredible Hulk, Fantastic Four and X Men comics.

The music of the sixties had provided us with the melodic Beatles, the hackneyed rock of the Rolling Stones, clever lyrics of the Kinks, the cute pop of the Monkees and Manfred Mann's lyrically zany blues numbers.

In the early seventies pop music was now growing bigger and more popular with so many new and expanding genres to explore. We had the Glam Rock era of course with loud, catchy, foot stomping pop anthems by the likes of David Bowie, T Rex, Sweet, Mud, Suzi Quatro and Slade. Plus, there was also the emerging heavy rock bands like Thin Lizzy, Black Sabbath, Kiss, Led Zeppelin, Iron Maiden, Alice Cooper and so many more.

Prog-Rock was also huge in the mid-seventies with all those album bands like Genesis, Uriah Heep, Yes, ELP, King Crimson, Hawkwind, Mike Oldfield and Pink Floyd.

There was also a burgeoning pub rock scene in London which produced so many great groups and stars. Doctor Feelgood, Eddie and the Hot Rods, Remus Down Boulevard, Nutz, Kilburn and the Highroads, Dogwatch, Kursaal Flyers and many more.

The first song that really did it for me was 'Wild Thing' by The Troggs around 1966. I can vividly remember standing in the kitchen of my grandad's old house in Grove Park and my Uncle Barry playing it to me on his new reel to reel, tape machine. Remember those big Akai spool tape machines? They were to a young kid like me something magical that could play you your favourite song on time and time again.

I was only eight years old at that time and I kept making my Uncle Barry play 'Wild Thing' over and over again. I don't know why but it struck something deep and primal inside of me that resonated and had gripped my mind and body completely and I remember thinking, 'Oh yeah Jim, this is definitely the best. I liked most of the pop music of that time but this song was something quite different to the usual, it just hit me square in the chest and vibrated within me. The Troggs themselves had a sort of physical 'on stage menace' to them as well. When I first saw The Troggs on Top Of The Pops they looked like gangsters or a mob of recently released criminals who'd taken up playing music. I just fucking lapped it up.

I have now since realised that this is the way I have subconsciously chosen many of my favourite bands over the last fifty odd years. If they played exciting and raunchy songs but also had the added bonus of looking mean and menacing too, I would take to them instantly.

Bands like Dr Feelgood for instance with the manic Wilko Johnson, machine gunning the audiences with his black Fender Stratocaster whilst zig zagging crazily across the stage. Partnered up with the broody looking frontman Lee Brilleaux on vocals who was always dressed in sweaty, beer stained suits, snapping his body and growling out vocals like a preacher with Tourette's with the whole band having an aggressive air of threat or malevolence to them.

Alice Cooper with the whole black mascara horror thing going on and appearing on TOTP waving a sword about, dressing up and using a guillotine on stage at his live shows with his incredibly catchy songs about teenage angst, school days. Almost as if Alice had written them for me personally and was lyrically emoting exactly how I felt as a struggling, shy, frustrated, hormone addled teenager struggling to grow up through confusing adolescence.

Then later came Killing Joke with their mighty guitar riffing sound and throbbing, tribal drums, spitting out post-apocalyptic anthems about the end of the world, fronted by the madman genius Jaz Coleman. The Stranglers are still one of my very favourites, all mean and moody and full of spiteful, misogynous, venomous and defiant lyrics and yet such well-crafted, exciting and memorable songs mixed up in melody and aggression. New Model Army with their fanatical, pikey looking, clog wearing, soap-dodging, devoted northern tribe of followers and their kick ass brand of gloriously rebellious, vengeful, angry yet memorable songs.

It is everything I ever wanted in any band that I would form to be like.

I wanted to be down to earth, gritty and angry yet with poignant lyrics and catchy singalong choruses that the fans would remember long after the gig and still be singing on their way home.

Right so where was I again?

Oh yeah, my small circle of friends in Dagenham.

There was Micky Petts, from a few doors down. He was a strange lad and went to a different school to me, somewhere called Richard Alibon, that I had no idea where it was. He loved playing football and so every evening after school, along with a few other local boys, we'd go to Heath Park to play footy with all the other young urchins on our Heath Park estate. Micky was good at it too and kept reminding everyone playing of 'the flash, the skill and the speed of the Alibon boy', as he dribbled and weaved his way past us with ease, the ball seemingly glued to his feet, and skilfully avoiding our crunching tackles, violent lunges and futile attempts to scythe the little fucker down.

There were a few local lads that met up on Heath Park or over the school playing field to play footy after school or at weekends and I loved it and dare I say it, I was pretty good little right winger too. So I had my band of footy mates yeah, but no proper mates yet.

My mum seemed anxious at that time that I needed a proper friend around the fourteen and fifteen year old mark, as I only had a few school friends to mix with at weekends or during half terms etc.

So one day, as I sat up at the dining room table drawing Spiderman or the Thing from Fantastic Four from out my Marvel comic collection, my mum told me that a neighbour woman that she'd recently gotten friendly with from across the road was bringing her only child over to meet me. He too was apparently bad at making friends and around my age too.

"Why are you telling us about this now, Jim?" I can almost hear you groan.

Because meeting this new friend, at that particular time in my life was probably the catalyst for steering me in a new direction. So please be patient.

This was in 1973.

The woolly headed boy that was brought over, somewhat reluctantly I might add, and into our living room to be introduced to me was a strange, ginger lad with pale skin which was littered with ginger freckles. He was thin and gangly and had a whiny voice and I found out later he had more teenage neurosis than me about his sad, lonely teenage life and his self-image.

His name was Malcolm Oliver and as I mentioned previously he was an only child. We got on okay but it was obviously a little awkward and tentative to start with but as luck would have it, he also shared a love of Marvel super hero comics, rock and pop music and sci-fi novels too. He was also very impressed with how good I was at drawing. We struck up a sort of friendship and I would often go over to his house some evenings during the week to talk about comics, favourite television shows, sci-fi novels and of course about our favourite bands.

We were both buying the latest pop singles with our weekly pocket money and slowly getting into the whole 70's music scene in general. As we grew older we started to go out to local pubs and to explore music venues and bands together.

As an only child Malc was spoilt rotten by his parents. He had his own TV in his bedroom and a stack, hi-fi system too. His parents seemed to give him endless amounts of cash to spend on records, tapes, comic books or gadgets, whereas I was lucky just to be getting a couple of quid in pocket money once a week.

So each time I'd go over to his house he would always seem to have a new gadget to show off or to have acquired the latest new album by Bowie, Alice Cooper, ELP, Roxy Music or whoever, whereas I could only afford to buy maybe two new singles per week or maybe an album if I saved up my pocket money.

I was very envious of him.

He also had both an acoustic guitar and an electric guitar with a tiny amplifier that his 'over generous' parents had bought for him and it wasn't even fucking Christmas.

I had only a cheap acoustic guitar which I struggled to keep tuned up and Malc had an electronic tuner to keep his two guitars in tune.

But we decided to learn how to play chords together and learn scales and such. I only really ever managed to grasp the basic open chords plus the 'A shape' and 'E shape' bar chords because it was all I needed. I couldn't play a guitar solo to save my life but I was becoming a reasonably, reliable rhythm guitarist. So together over many months we practised and taught each other basic guitar chords and soon we felt more capable of trying to write our very own songs.

Anyway as we started writing these self-penned songs with both of us on guitar we gradually began to get the hang of it. I'd be the basic rhythm guitarist and Malc would pick out the melodies and do the guitar solos. The songs that we wrote together were basically rock songs with creative and unpredictable song lyrics about anything from crime to the supernatural or about love or heartbreak. The guitar riffs were primitive but we slowly began to improve and a year or so later we weren't half bad. Well I thought so anyway. By 1975 we had written maybe a dozen rock songs and we would record them onto cassette tapes and so I suggested to him one day that we could maybe start thinking about forming a band? To my surprise and disappointment Malc told me he wasn't keen on playing our songs to anybody just yet. So when I asked him why he gave me a convoluted answer about us at least waiting until we'd both mastered our instruments properly. A ridiculous argument, I thought, because surely being in a band was more about enthusiasm, creativity and energy over technical ability, right?

But he would not be swayed.

I remember getting a small and very basic, second hand drum kit for my younger brother to play on in our new group to see what the songs sounded like with a drum beat to them. On most Saturday nights in the mid-seventies my parents liked to go out with their friends to have a drink and see shows and let their hair down a bit. They were semi-regulars at the Circus Tavern in Purfleet and they would get me to babysit my two brothers and little sister (who had recently arrived in July of 1970) while they went out on the lash. So when my parents left I would call up Malc and tell him to bring his guitar and amplifier over and we would set up the drum kit, amps and guitars in my parent's living room and we would bang out our crude self-penned songs loudly plus a couple of cover versions too. I still have some of those living room jam sessions taped onto old cassettes somewhere too. I took most of the lead vocals as well as rhythm guitar and thought that we sounded really good. We were loud, raw and raucous and a bit rough around the edges but full of passion and energy. How the neighbours put up with us I'll never know.

True fact: David Essex's aunt (Mrs Cook) lived two doors down from us and I think she did actually complain once to my mum about the noise, so that's how fucking awesomely loud we were if she could hear us two houses away.

Some of the songs we wrote had titles like 'Times are Hard', "Limelight', 'Detroit Kid' and 'I Wanna Be Free.'

Like I said I still have a few of them on cassette tapes and they do make me smile whenever I dig them out to have a listen to if I'm feeling nostalgic. Early versions of punk songs really you could say and so maybe I was slightly ahead of the curve back then without really knowing it?

So that was really my initial first foray into trying to form a band and for a few months I actually thought I might convince my brother and Malc into becoming a real band and to start looking for gigs. Yet after a while my brother got bored and caught the gambling bug and started going to the Romford dogs religiously every Saturday night with his own mates and Malc's interest in playing guitar waned, as he moved onto other new hobbies such as photography and travelling. It was annoying to me but the passion and determination I felt would only grow stronger in the coming years.

So my old mate Malcolm Oliver was probably the initial catalyst for stirring up the whole 'real possibility' of the 'actually being in a band' thing for me back then. A few years later I asked him if he would take some photos of The Ejected for me which he kindly agreed to do. It is his photographs that we used for the cover of 'A Touch of Class' and for the back sleeve of 'Spirit of Rebellion', so in a way I sort of included him in the band thing eventually.

Then in July 1975 I left school and had to get a job.

My world suddenly changed.

My first job was an office job as Assistant Purchasing Clerk at a shipping supplies company in Canning Town, literally on a small industrial trading estate down the road from the famous Bridge House music venue.

So every weekday I travelled from Dagenham Heathway to West Ham on the tube wearing a suit, shirt and tie.

It was a small firm with about eight warehouse guys and about fifteen office staff. I was still a fairly shy seventeen year old remember and suddenly being thrust into an office environment where I had to answer the phone to suppliers, order stock, deal with reps and progress orders came as a real shock to me at first. Yet after a couple of years there I really came out of my shell. The office staff eventually grew to love me and became like an extended family to me. And once I got used to the daily commute, the 9 to 5 routine and work/life culture, I started to grow up a bit. This was also where I learned about drinking at lunchtimes because a few of the older office blokes would go to the pub around the corner called The Durham Arms (literally about a hundred yards down the road from The Canning Town Bridge House) and eventually one day, they coaxed me into going along. Lunchtime drinking was a new experience for me, and many was the afternoon I'd stagger back to the office, after a couple of lager shandy's feeling dizzy, tired or a bit sick.

I was a lightweight back then but slowly I got used to it and learned about buying rounds for colleagues in those lunch time sessions too.

The best thing about working was payday (obviously) which was once a month and that was usually when I went a bit mad. Whenever I got paid I was always useless at managing my money. So on most paydays I'd go into Canning Town and draw out my meagre monthly salary at Barclays Bank and then hit the Melody Man record shop up the road a bit in Plaistow, to buy myself a load of new vinyl albums or singles which made me feel like life was worth living again at last. In '76 I was going through a heavy rock phase so I'd be buying albums by the likes of AC/DC, Thin Lizzy, New York Dolls, Kiss and Uriah Heep but New Wave music and Punk was also just getting started around that time too and so I would also be buying albums by the likes of Ultravox, the Ramones, Patti Smith, Blondie, The Damned, Sex Pistols and the Stranglers.

During this time one of my old school friends that I had managed to stay in touch with got himself a job at Barking town hall, as a trainee civil engineer or something, so we started travelling to work together each morning. His name was Steve Sandbrook and we had two things in common: our love for music and football. I had recently started going over to watch Dagenham FC play each Saturday afternoon and some of the midweek home games too at Victoria Road. So Steve decided that he would tag along with me whenever his team West Ham were playing away.

So this was the '76/77' season and the Daggers had a decent team for a change and were doing quite well with great players like Dennis Moore, Terry Harris, Ian Hutley, Mal Harkins, John Borland and my old history teacher Neville Fox. Anyway the Daggers made it all the way to the FA Trophy final at Wembley that season. So we got excited and decided that we just had to go. So Steve volunteered to go and queue up early for our Wembley tickets at the ground on Saturday morning as he only lived around the corner from the Victoria Road ground and that I should pop round in the afternoon to pick my two tickets up from him (one for my youngest brother too who was seven at that time and that I had just started taking along to watch the Saturday home games).

Later that day I went round as agreed to collect my tickets from him. Steve lived with his parents and two younger brothers in Sterry Road, Dagenham just two streets away from me.

I remember going into the front room to chat excitedly about our upcoming big day at Wembley and Steve's brother Gary joining us to chat about it too. Gary was a year younger than us and a Chelsea supporter (groans all round) but this was way back when being a Chelsea fan wasn't the plain sailing thing it is these days. Anyway the three of us were sitting around the family hi-fi and listening to albums when I get around to mentioning my love of this New Wave/Punk music and how I had bought albums by bands like The Ramones, Stranglers, Wire and Ultravox. Steve wasn't much interested as he has always been a diehard Yes, ELP, Frank Zappa and Genesis kind of guy but to my surprise Gary had heard of them and he had a copy of the Ultravox debut album too. So we got talking about all these new wave and punk bands and our mutual love of the (now legendary) John Peel late night radio show. I had not met or really spoken to Gary much before this and you all know that moment in life when you meet a kindred spirit right? Who totally gets it and is into all the same bands and artists, old and new, that you are. So from that chance meeting on that Saturday afternoon in May '77 we fast became best mates.

We became inseparable and began going to gigs all over London in search of new upcoming bands. At weekends we would go into Romford and search all the local record stores for new vinyl. Every other Saturday morning we'd take the tube up to Oxford Street in London because the big West End record stores always seemed to stock the new releases quicker than Romford or Barking and even a few of the back street independent record stores did too. So we would doggedly hunt down the latest single or album that we had heard and liked on the John Peel Show during the previous weeks.

We saw many great bands too. The Adverts, Wire, Ultravox, UK Subs, The Stranglers, Undertones, Damned, The Cockney Rejects, Rezillos, The Passions, The Skids, XTC and so many more.

We had started to become regulars at the Bridge House, Canning Town too and even saw one of Depeche Mode's first ever gigs there, supporting Fad Gadget.

The Murphy family ran the Bridge House (Terry Murphy and his sons Glen the boxer and London' Burning actor and Darren the Wasted Youth band member) and they would book a wide spectrum of acts regardless of musical genre. So during any given week you could see bands ranging from rock. blues, punk, ska, mod and indie.

They were totally into bringing up and coming new bands as well as the standard pub rock bands. There was always something on at the pub to suit mostly everyone's tastes to see and the beer was decently priced too, not the watered down, inflated priced shit you'd get in London at the Marquee club or Rock Garden. It was heaven for us too because it was just seven stops on the tube from Dagenham Heathway to West Ham station and then a five minute walk up to the venue.

One night Gary and I went to see The Jags play at The Bridge House because they were in the charts with their single 'Back of My Hand (I Got Your Number)' and we got quite pissed. We came out after the gig was over and I shinned up the metal post of a nearby road traffic sign with my trusty black marker pen and scrawled UK Subs on the white background of the traffic sign. Then a voice shouted at us from the shadows across the road where we suddenly spotted a parked police car. The cop rolled down the side window and yelled at us to 'Come over there' and I shouted 'Bollocks, run Gal!" and I started to leg it up the road with one of the coppers chasing after me while Gary had apparently just walked over to the police car obediently. Stephenson Street was a long old road, and I easily outran the copper because I was fitter and a faster back then. But with all the beer inside me I started to flag after five hundred yards or so and decided to crouch down and hide behind a wall at the top of the road, as the alcohol was getting to me a bit and I was out of puff. The two coppers were back in the car with Gary sat in the back seat and came driving after me, they whizzed past my hiding place at first and I breathed a sigh of relief. But then they realised I was not anywhere to be seen up ahead in the road that led to West Ham tube station so they turned around and came back to find me panting hard behind the wall. They threw me in the back of the car roughly next to Gary and drove us to Plaistow police station. Then they chucked us in a cell together and charged the two of us with being drunk and disorderly and me with criminal damage. Still being quite pissed we were laughing and humming Z cars and The Sweeney theme tunes in the cell. Eventually they slung us out at around two in the morning telling us that we had to night bus it all the way back home to Dagenham.

We appeared at Bow Road magistrates court a few weeks later which was an anxious first time for the both of us and we got fined. I remember the magistrate telling me to take my hands out of my pockets when I took the stand and quite weirdly the cop giving the court evidence and reading aloud from his note book that I shouted 'Bollocks, run Gal', which made me laugh and I think the magistrate stuck an extra ten quid onto my fine for it, which was eventually £60 which was lot of dosh back then.

So, me and Gary had definitely caught the 'Punk Rock thing' big time back then. During the week we'd often finish work, go home, scoff down dinner, get changed and then rush back out to travel out to music venues all over the capital like the Marquee, Lyceum, Electric Ballroom, Hope & Anchor, Thomas a Beckett, Ruskin Arms, Half Moon, Bridge House and so many more. We lived and breathed punk and new wave music. We especially loved the UK Subs and would try and go see them whenever they played in London. One night they were playing at the Queen Mary University over in Mile End. I had quite recently bought myself a pair of very tight, black, bondage trousers and decided to debut them at this particular Subs gig. We went inside and watched the support act but during the opening number of Subs set a crowd of East end skins piled into the venue and started to beat up the audience (I later found out they thought all UK Subs fans were Chelsea supporters) and so the gig was abandoned. As the skins chased everyone into the street outside me and Gary found ourselves running for our lives, which was not fucking easy in tight bloody bondage trousers with straps linking the legs together. Luckily we made it to Mile End tube station without getting our heads kicked in and I wisely binned the bondage strides the very next day. From then on it was jeans and steel toe capped work boots for us at gigs. Bondage trousers are fine to pose in but fucking useless to run in.

So it was only a matter of time before I started to talk to Gary about forming our own band. I had an electric guitar and a 30 watt combo amplifier by this time (courtesy of a £77 tax rebate six months after I had started working) and Gary and his brother owned a couple of acoustic guitars and a cheap electric guitar. I was a pretty decent rhythm guitarist by this time and Gary was one of those naturally gifted bastards that could play almost any instrument he picked up. I asked Gary if he could play bass? He shrugged at me and said maybe, so for that upcoming Christmas he asked his parents if they could get him a bass guitar and they did. Steve, as it turned out, had a flair for playing the drums too we soon discovered when one Saturday night (when my parents were off out seeing Jimmy Jones or Mike Reid up at the Circus Tavern) and I was back on babysitting duty.

I invited Steve and Gary round and set up the combo amp, second hand drum kit in the lounge again and we jammed a bit before doing a few covers of Alice Cooper's 'Eighteen', 'Steppin' Stone' by the Monkees, the Sex Pistols 'Anarchy in the UK' and a very punk version of 'House of the Rising Sun' (the old Animals classic). We sounded pretty decent too and so over the coming months, Gary and I began to write a few punky songs of our own with titles like 'Tank', 'Criminal Mind' and 'Commuter Society'.

But alas Steve wasn't really into it as a 'serious thing' and so we were back to square one. It was around that time we bought a rhythm box so that we'd have a decent beat to compose and write all our new songs too. After a while we realised that if we seriously wanted to be in a band we needed to start doing things properly.

So it was decided that we should advertise for a female singer to front the band as neither of us felt confident enough of our own vocal skills, especially while we were both playing guitar and bass, so we thought let's get a bird in to sing and front the band. Our rather skewed reasoning being that back then bands who had female singer's in them seemed to pull in more punters at gigs. We also needed a decent drummer too as none of our mates were interested in punk rock or drumming for us.

So it was time to turn to the classified 'Musicians Wanted' ads at the back of the music papers like Sounds and Melody Maker.

This meant putting in adverts for a female singer and a decent drummer.

Since starting work I had started buying Sounds religiously, every Wednesday morning on my way to work, because they were championing the whole 'punk and new wave' thing that was now sweeping the country and they also had this young writer, reviewer and journalist called Garry Bushell, on the staff, who was into helping young, up and coming bands by doing interviews, reviewing gigs and giving out helpful advice too.

So over the following months I put ads in all the music paper classifieds sections for a female punk vocalist and for a dedicated punk rock drummer too.

Hopefully we would be on our way now.

(Ps. Dagenham lost 2 - 1to fucking Scarborough in that 1977 FA Trophy final at Wembley. It was such a disappointment after the Daggers were one nil up for most of the game and yet lost to two jammy Scarborough goals in the final five minutes. Well that's how I remember it anyway).

Chapter two

We auditioned so many female vocalists over the ensuing months and finding the perfect one was so bloody difficult. It was mostly because there were pretty ones that were not punky looking enough but could sing and punky ones who looked great but were crap at singing. The few that could sing we would hang out with for a while in pubs or at gigs to see how we all got on but usually it just fizzled out in the end and got very frustrating.

Then one day we found her.

Her name was Dawn Payne and she was originally from a place called Thame, in Oxfordshire but she told us that she had left home to come and live in London in a dodgy bedsit in Tufnell Park in the hope of joining or forming a punk band.

We arranged to meet her outside the Embankment tube station one night and when we got there we spotted Dawn straight away.

She had blonde spiky hair, leopard print skirt, studded leather jacket and biker boots. A proper punkette at last. She was small and a bit short sighted (and refused to wear glasses out of vanity she later confided in me) but she looked great and she knew and loved all the same new up and coming punk bands as us. We went into a pub near the station and drank, laughed and chatted for hours. She even told us that she wrote her own song lyrics and had brought along a pile of self-penned lyrics that she had written to show us.

Dawn had plenty of attitude as well as creative ideas and she also appeared to like us too, so we decided to audition her that very weekend.

Even though we still didn't have a drummer yet we decided to rehearse with Dawn anyway and she came over to Dagenham to audition with us at rehearsal studio close to where we lived and we used our little rhythm box plugged into an amp as a temporary drummer. Everything went surprisingly well and so Dawn was our new vocalist. Over the ensuing weeks we rehearsed regularly and using some of her song lyrics and mine together with my guitar riffs we wrote a handful of new songs pretty quickly too. Songs like 'Back Street Abortion', 'Snyde Family', 'Machine Gun', 'What Am I Gonna Do (with me)' and 'Football Song'.

We also got her singing some of our songs too which she seemed to cope with admirably. Her voice was loud, aggressive, edgy and very punk rock.

So we decided to call our new band Dawn Patrol.

At one of our rehearsal sessions a young local guy came in from the rehearsal room next door and started chatting to us. He said he liked our raw, energetic sound but wondered why we had no drummer? When we explained to him that it was hard finding good punk drummers he suddenly offered to play drums for us. We learned that his name was Joe Silverman and he sang in a pub covers band called 'Elected' but was a frustrated drummer at heart and he even owned his own drum kit. He was a local lad too living in Hornchurch, so we offered him an audition and he was not brilliant but better than nothing. He also told us that he had a mate with a four track recording studio in his back garden that we could use to record a cheap demo tape.

Now demo tapes were all the rage back then and it was the best way of getting your band a gig or even possibly a record deal.

Record three or four songs in a studio and get it onto a cassette tape along with all the information and contact numbers of the band and send it out to all the music venues and independent record labels.

That was our strategy anyway.

So one Sunday we met up and herded all our equipment into the back garden shed/studio of Joe's milkman mate, somewhere near Rainham train station in Essex and recorded and mixed four songs in about six hours. I still have that demo tape to this day and although it is very raw it is very full of energy but really is quite bad. The songs we put on it were 'Football Song', 'Snyde Family', 'Commuter Society' and a punk version of 'Steppin' Stone'.

I suppose that we were chuffed with it at the time plus none of us had any real experience of recording studios of mixing desks, so it was probably all very exciting to us.

Anyway we now had a demo tape that meant we could try and get Dawn Patrol a few gigs. We actually landed two gigs in a very short time after sending out a load of our copied demo tape cassettes. The first wasn't actually a gig as such but was an offer to play two songs on a 'New Local Bands Talent Night' at the Zero Six club in Southend.

This got us very excited.

A little too excited as I recall.

I had convinced a few of my work colleagues to come and see us play for moral support. I should mention at this point I had changed job and was now working at a company in Dagenham called Wholesale Fittings (where I stayed for 22 years believe it or not) as a warehouseman which I was much more comfortable with. So no more wearing a suit or bloody tie to work, just regular jeans and tee shirts and steel toe capped boots. It was literally a ten minute walk from my parent's house too and better wages.

Anyway, a load of us descended on the Zero Six club in Southend-on-Sea on a rainy Monday night. As me, Gary, Dawn and Joe were very nervous we drank a few too many lager tops and ciders before it was our turn to go on. Dawn gave it her all up on stage and I can only vaguely remember playing as I was more than a bit pissed that night. I do recall that Dawn was very feisty, angry and aggressive and also tanked up on a few too many ciders and at the end of our two song set (I have no idea which two songs we performed) she hurled the microphone down in a punk rock Johnny Rotten style, as her big punk finale before leaving the stage.

Ten minutes later a couple of management lads approached us demanding fifty quid because Dawn had broken the microphone. We had to have a quick whip round between all our mates to pay them otherwise they were threatening to seize our guitars as collateral unless we coughed up.

So not a big success.

But at the same time, very Punk Rock!

Undeterred we had ourselves a proper second gig to play at Walthamstow Youth centre and we were headlining it too. The majority of that audience turned out to be kids that night mostly between the ages of about twelve to eighteen (I suppose the clue was in Youth Centre, duh!) but it was still exciting for us until we got news from our drummer Joe that his covers band had a paying pub gig that same night. He did come along to our gig in Walthamstow but upon learning that we were not the support band he fucked off early to go do his paying pub gig and left us stranded without a drummer. Luckily though we persuaded the support bands drummer to stand in for Joe and he did a far better job than Joe could ever have done and we went down quite well. Whilst also managing to stay at least semi-sober.

So Joe was out.

A few weeks later we auditioned a young guy called Steve who'd answered one of our music paper adverts. He had a bit of a stutter but was a really good drummer and with his shaved head, Harrington jacket and Doc Marten's really looked the part.

At that time we had started rehearsing at a north London studio called Demon studios and the rehearsal rooms were all fitted out with powerful, Marshall stack amps and a big drum kit and so suddenly we were using decent equipment, which started to make Dawn Patrol sound very tight, fast, punky and loud.

It was everything that I had hoped for and envisioned and that I ever wanted to be part of. I recall one time after a particularly brilliant rehearsal we came out of the studio and Gary pointed to our reflections in the store window on the opposite side of the road saying 'We even look like a famous punk band'. We all followed his stare at our leather jacketed reflections across the street and began laughing and had to agree that we really did look like the dogs bollocks too.

So around this time (1980) Dawn and I were starting to get quite close. I had only ever had two girlfriends before and both relationships had lasted no longer than a few weeks before fizzling out. (I would tell you all the background stories as to why I messed up with the beautiful brown eyed Karen and the slightly religious and naive Jill but I think I'd come out looking pathetic and inept in both disastrous stories. So I'll skip it if it's all the same to you ha ha).

So Dawn was staying over with me in my parent's house at weekends and a few nights during the week too. She was a bit anxious and scared of some predatory guy who was living in a rented room at her bedsit house over in Tufnell Park, who had apparently been hassling her a bit. So after explaining this situation to my mum she finally agreed that Dawn could sleep in my bed as long as I slept on the bedroom floor. So as the old saying goes one thing led to another and things happened between the two of us at night whilst all my family was asleep and I was gradually starting to get romantic feelings for her.

"Aw bless," I hear you all saying.

So not long after Steve joined the band I rang Dawn up one night when she was at her bedsit to check things were okay and to chat about some band stuff too and she casually mentioned that Steve was over at her place.

I suddenly just freaked out (with petulant jealousy and anger) demanding to know what they were up to? Dawn insisted that they were just trying to write new song ideas for the band but I wasn't having any of it. I accused her of lying and even flat out asked her if she was she shagging Steve? Dawn denied it but in a fit of idiotic rage I told her angrily that I was quitting the band and then slammed the phone down on her. I fully expected her to ring me back straight away and to apologise (though god knows what for) and reassure me of her love and beg me to reconsider.

It never happened.

In thirty seconds I had fucked everything up.

Big time.

I had been so stupid.

So then I'd had to call up Gary and explain to him why I was quitting the band. He was not impressed. He said that he was so happy that we were finally a solid four piece and on the brink of actually getting somewhere that I should ring Dawn and apologise. I told him sheepishly that if he wanted to continue being in Dawn Patrol I wouldn't stand in his way and would respect his decision but there was no way I could swallow my stupid pride and apologise to her. Gary told me that he would sleep on it and let me know what his decision was the next day.

In the end Gary decided to quit the band too and stick with me to start over.

I was so relieved. I was a stupid bastard I know. Dawn Patrol could have been such a huge success if I had just swallowed my stupid insecurities and pride and been professional about it all. Dawn was a great asset and I had cut off my nose just to spite my face.

Dawn and Steve carried on Dawn Patrol (without me and Gary) and went on to release a 12 inch EP. It's really good too and I have a copy somewhere. As far as I know it was their only release. There is a track called 'Prisoner' on the EP that is fucking superb in my opinion and also a version of 'What Am I Gonna Do' which Dawn and I had written together so, if you were wondering why there are two versions that is why. Both The Ejected and Dawn Patrol have recorded versions of it.

I have many fond memories of Dawn too, some good and some bad, she was never dull or boring and always creative. She could be so funny too but would often get us into a lot of trouble whenever she'd had a few too many ciders. She was a true punkette.

So no more female vocalists for us!

We were well into 1980 now and the 'Oi and street punk' thing was happening all over the country and starting to take off. It was an offshoot of punk which was more about aggression and less about the melody and was played very fast and very loud. So Gary and I decided we could handle that and so we started to advertise for yet another new drummer and vowed to stay a three piece from now on and sharing the vocal duties between us. We also set about writing more terrace chant type songs and street anthems with catchy choruses that suited our rough, shouty and aggressive male voices.

We also made a conscious effort to bulk up a bit and so we started weight training every Monday evening after work at a gym in the local swimming baths complex that had just been built. It was to boost our confidence and to try and make us not only physically stronger but to try and appear more intimidating and hard looking. After each workout session on the various bench and pulley weight machines, which we did in our jeans with our tee shirts off (no Lycra posing back in those days) we'd adjourn to a nice little pub around the corner called The Three Travellers.

The Three Travellers was a bit old fashioned but we liked it even though they sold mild and had bar billiards. It was also the less disreputable of the three pubs located at the far end of Dagenham at the junction of Heathway, Whalebone Lane and Wood lane. The other two pubs being The Merry Fiddlers and the Ship and Anchor.

Anyway it was whilst sitting in this pub one particular evening shortly after the whole Dawn Patrol fiasco that we were chatting about how many punk gigs we'd been to and how often it was that some of the punks outside the tube stations near to the venues or even outside the music venue itself were always going up to people and asking "Have you got 10p?" to help contribute to them getting into the gig or for train or bus fare home.

So that's where I came up with the idea of writing a song about it.

So our most famous Ejected song got written after a weight training session in an old man's pub whilst we were moaning about punks and skins trying to ponce money off of us at gigs.

So every time I do a gig I am constantly getting asked or shouted at 'Hey Jim, have you got 10p?' and I still always manage a wry smile before replying 'Nah, not me'.

Chapter three

We finally got ourselves a good new drummer shortly after that and I had also come up with a new band name.

The Ejected.

Because I wanted a name that suited the kind of raw, gritty, angry and defiant singalong punk and Oi band that we really wanted to be. I also thought it would sound good beside other great punk band names like the UK Subs, Cockney Rejects, Exploited and Angelic Upstarts.

So that was the new band name.

During this time me and Gary were still going out and watching new bands play and one night we travelled south of the river to Deptford to see an all-girl, indie band that we quite liked called the Androids of Mu.

The support act at this gig was another all-female outfit called The Gymslips who as the name suggested came on stage wearing gymslips, school ties, white shirts and even straw boaters. As we watched these feisty looking birds blast through their set I kept staring at the bass player who was kitted up in full St. Trinian's outfit including stockings, suspenders and high heels (Dirty Schoolgirl style). When they finished their set I mentioned to Gary that I liked the look of the sexy bassist and he admitted that he quite fancied the Gymslips lead guitarist.

We then watched the Androids of Mu play and enjoyed their quirky brand of original, anarcho-indie rock and afterwards we got chatting to the Android's drummer Cozmic and keyboardist Suze up at the bar and when we told them that we had travelled all the way from Dagenham, over in East London to come see them play they mentioned that that's where their support band the Gymslips were from.

So on the way out I noticed a pile of flyers that The Gymslips had left behind by the door with info about the band on it, including a phone number at the bottom with a 593 prefix which I instantly recognised as a Dagenham number.

So the following day I rang that number up and got chatting to Anita (the sexy St. Trinian's clad bass player that I fancied) and I told her that we had seen The Gymslips play last night and that we were in punk band and lived in Dagenham. Anita seemed impressed and chatty and I was enjoying chatting her up so much I let slip that Gary fancied the guitarist Paula and also that I fancied her and she laughed and replied that the four of us should meet up for a drink one night, even cheekily remarking to me that neither she nor Paula had had a shag in ages.

So we met them up at her local pub a few nights later, which turned out to be the Railway Tavern up by Dagenham East tube station (it's a Tesco Extra now).

We all got on like a house on fire and so I started dating Anita and Gary started seeing Paula.

A few months later I moved into Anita's one bedroom flat because it was like heaven to me at that time. There were six of us at home and us four kids were all older now, so it was a pretty crowded at the house. Anita had a couple of electric guitars, a bass, several amps, microphones and an interesting record collection. She was also ten years older than me and so she was responsible for turning the boy into a man if you know what I mean?

We got married in May of '81.

Gary was my best man and Paula was one of Anita's bridesmaids.

The new Ejected drummer was a guy called Dave Owen from East Ham in East London and not only was he an excellent drummer he was hilarious too. He also drank and smoked which has always been an Ejected prerequisite.

So now we rehearsed like mad and got the songs tightened up and also wrote a whole bunch more to boot. I remember writing East End Kids around that time and suddenly feeling more confident in The Ejected and our new strong and exciting punk/Oi songs and sound.

Once again though we found out that our drummer Dave Owen also played drums for a local pub covers band called 'Drivin' South' and so we still had the whole 'gigs not clashing' thing to worry about again for fuck's sake.

Anyway by this time I was quite pally with Garry Bushell over at Sounds music paper who made himself quite accessible in those days, so sometimes I'd ring him up at the Sounds office to ask him questions like which venues should we send our demo tapes to if we wanted a gig? He was well in with the Cockney Rejects and even had his own south London Oi band called The Gonads going on too and was really promoting the punk/Oi/street punk scene that was springing up all over the place in Britain.

Bands like Criminal Class, The Business, Last Resort, Angela Rippon's Bum, 4 Skins, Peter and the Test Tube Babies and so many more.

So I learned from Garry Bushell that he was behind a compilation album featuring these types of bands and that he had been championing and released 'The Oi Album!' and was planning a follow up called 'Carry On Oi!' which he was currently putting together. So he asked me to send him a copy The Ejected's latest demo tape (that we had recently recorded in a studio at Clapham Junction with Dave Owen on drums) and he'd see if we could be included on the album.

The new demo tape was a big improvement and we were very pleased with how good it had turned out. It sounded great, we included the tracks 'East End Kids', 'Factory Song', 'Gang Warfare,' and 'Have You Got 10p?'. Sadly though, I no longer seem to have a copy of that demo tape.

Anyway Garry Bushell liked it enough to ask us to go up to Matrix Studios, a posh professional studio complex up in West London, to record two songs for his new 'Carry on Oi!' album. My few remaining memories of that day of recording at Matrix studios were of Dave Owen taking fucking ages to sort out his drum kit and fucking around trying to get the right acoustic sound to them with the over fussy, sound engineer. I remember that me and Gary fucked off to a café around the corner to kill time and have ourselves a tasty fry up. Later while we were listening back to the two songs we had recorded which were 'East End Kids' and 'What Am I Gonna do' the sound engineer guy informed us that Bryan Ferry was in the next door studio and did we want to hear what was going on in there? We said yeah and so he flipped a switch on the mixing desk to let us eavesdrop on what Ferry was doing. I'll never forget hearing Bryan Ferry mucking about in the vocal booth and singing the lyrics to 'Planet Earth' by Duran Duran.

Anyway we recorded our two songs and then we were told that the mixing of all the tracks would be at a later date and if we wanted to come along to advise or listen we were welcome. Me and Gary decided that we would go along to hear the mix of our songs a few weeks later. The two guys mixing the album were quite surprised (and a little crestfallen I think) that we had bothered to show up and offer our input, as none of the other bands had been that bothered. It was a good job we did too because when they played us back their final mix of our two songs it sounded fucking awful, their mix made us sound like we had recorded our two tracks down a wind tunnel or something. I had a feeling that the two yuppie looking sound engineers were not the biggest fans of Punk or Oi music and that their hearts weren't really in it. In the end me and Gary had to put them straight and we insisted that they do another remix of our two songs to at least make us sound less wimpy or distorted. Even now when I do take a listen to that 'Carry On Oi' album I think that those two sound guys still sabotaged our tracks after we left because the sound quality of The Ejected on that compilation still sounds a bit naff to me.

Yet I was so proud when the album came out and I finally got to hold a physical copy in my hands with a photo of us on the back sleeve. It is a feeling I have never grown bored or tired of. Whenever I have created something like a single, album or a novel and gotten the physical copies sent to me I always find it to be one of the most thrilling of feelings in my life and I always will.

We were gradually playing a lot more smaller gigs and venues around London at the time and now that we had a good drummer and were also getting a few decent live gig reviews in Sounds too. We regularly played at a club called Skunx which was a weekly designated punk night at the Blue Coat Boy pub in Islington and seemed to be popular with London's punk and skinhead regulars. We played a gig at Hammersmith Clarendon supporting Manufactured Romance (who had a big indie hit with 'Time Of My Life' at the time) and we even played the famous 100 club in Oxford Street as support for the 4 Skins. Our reputation for playing raw, gritty but catchy punk anthems was building slowly. Our audiences were heavily skinhead loaded and I remember that Dave was not happy about that aspect of it all, mostly because he looked and dressed like a rocker with his long hair, beard and leather jacket. Me and Gary, however, were quite happy to have anyone show up at all to see us play but as each gig passed we noticed that Dave got seemingly less and less enthusiastic about our small hard core skinhead following.

It was around this time that I started sending out copies of our demo tape to all the well-known independent record companies that I believed might be interested in The Ejected and I was getting both positive and negative feedback from them.

Stiff records politely declined I remember but not because they disliked us at all but just because they thought we were not their type of band but wished us well anyway.

No Future records sent me a letter back as did Secret records, both basically saying that they could release our demo tracks as they were as an EP but were not willing or interested in shelling out any more money to put us back into a decent studio to record a proper new single which pissed me off because they were just trying to hedge their bets and not trusting us to be an 'economically viable' or 'popular' as a band. I still have their 'snidey' rejection letters taped into my old Ejected scrapbook.

Then I remember the morning that it finally happened for us.

I got a phone call from a guy called Simon Edwards at Riot City Records, up in Bristol, who I had sent a copy of our demo to. He already had Vice Squad, Abrasive Wheels, Chaos UK, The Varukers and Chaotic Dischord on his label.

I remember trying to sound cool talking to him but inside my heart was pounding with excitement. Simon told me that he loved 'Have You Got 10p?' and that he wanted to put it out as a single. He liked the other tracks on our demo tape too. He basically told me that if we signed with his label and put out 'Have You Got 10p' as a single and it sold well then he'd let us record an album too. It sounded like a fantastic offer but I kept my voice as calm as possible and informed him that I needed to consult with the rest of the band first and that I'd get back to him. We ended the call and as soon as I had put the phone down I did cartwheels and forward rolls across the bed and was punching the air and shouting 'Yes' over and over. Anita who was still in the bed at the time was staring at me like I'd gone crazy. Once I had calmed down a bit I explained the phone conversation to her and she seemed happy enough for me but as she had been recently sacked from the Gymslips it was obviously a hard time for her.

I rang Gary first with the exciting news of Riot City's offer and like me he was well chuffed about it.

When I rang Dave Owen about it he informed me rather soberly that he did not want to be in The Ejected any more. Apparently his other band had quite a few shows laid on and he said that he felt he needed to commit fully to them.

What shit news!

Right after getting the best fucking news of my life.

And a record deal.

The prick!

He even reckoned that his southern rock boogie band would be destined for better things than The Ejected.

The cheeky cunt!

Where are Drivin' South now eh? I've not seen or heard anything by them in like…EVER!

So I remember swallowing my anger and wishing him well and putting the phone down and immediately thinking…FUCK!

Chapter four

So we set about the whole process of advertising and auditioning for another fucking drummer yet again.

In the meantime we hadn't said anything to Simon Edwards about our knucklehead drummer's sudden resignation because I didn't want to jeopardise our big chance of recording our first single.

I had a work colleague at the time named Mick Robinson who played drums in a band called The Regulators and he was a nice guy. He lived in Southend-on-Sea (and still does) and after I'd explained our 'urgently needed' drummer situation to him, he kindly agreed to step in and help us out with recording the single. With pressure growing from Simon Edwards up at Riot City, I got us booked into Goldust recording studio in Bexley Heath to record our debut single.

In August of '82 we recorded the now legendary 'Have You Got 10p?' single with two tracks on the B-side 'Class of 82' and 'One Of The Boys' and Mick Robinson did us proud but alas was not free to join The Ejected for gigs at that time.

We did for a short period have a young Pakistani lad called Andy Spiers playing drums for us at a couple of gigs during this time but he was based in Bushey, Watford, so travelling with his kit proved a big problem as he didn't drive. He did the gigs where we were allowed to use the headlining bands' drum kit but in the end we came to the mutual agreement that we should part ways.

I did the sleeve design and artwork for the 'Have You Got 10p' single as Simon Edwards had agreed that I would be given free rein to do all future Ejected artwork. He was well happy with the single which got released and I recall him telling me a few weeks later that it had sold around five thousand copies. It made the UK Independent charts and even climbed into the top ten amongst such esteemed company as Depeche Mode, Dead Kennedys, UB40 and Yazoo.

Another proud moment for me was when John Peel played it on his radio show and afterwards said "A bit of a classic that," which was high praise indeed from the great man and it really pleased me. Especially after all the many years I that had been tuning into his late night show to hear him playing all my favourite bands like UK Subs, Stranglers, Undertones, etc.

It really began to feel like The Ejected, were finally beginning to make it after so many years of struggling.

We finally managed to find yet another good drummer after many long and awful auditions.

Paul Griffiths was to be the new and permanent member.

He was into punk music and also looked the part. He smoked JPS cigarettes and loved a few beers. Paul was a local lad too living in a flat in Ilford and by day he worked as a vending machine filler.

Simon Edwards agreed to let us do an album shortly after that and so in November 1982 we went into Scarf Studios in Bromley-by-Bow to record A Touch Of Class. We now had plenty of songs in our set which included the likes of 'Young Tribes Of England', 'Fast 'n' Loud', 'I'm Gonna Get A Gun', 'Man Of War', 'Football Song' 'Mr Muggins', 'England Ain't Dead', 'Gang Warfare' and a re-recorded version of 'Have You Got 10p? (with 'real arse'ole' instead of 'poor old soul') and 'East End Kids' too.

All of which have become firm favourites with our fans over the years.

The production and sound engineer on that first album was a young guy called Mark Lewis but we chipped in with how it should be mixed too and so it was more a collaboration really. We hurriedly banged it out in just three frenetic but exciting days because Simon Edwards insisted that he was on a tight budget. We didn't care, we just did the best we could and were very proud of the end result. It was fast, loud, ballsy, aggressive and raw. Most of the songs on it have very catchy choruses too which is something I always aim for when writing Ejected songs. It also had a real, down to earth street punk sound. My only slight complaint about it is that there are a few too many songs on it but as I said at the time we were really enjoying ourselves and didn't care. We just wanted to make it the best that we could.

It got released with my sleeve design and idea of using my old mate Malcolm Oliver (remember him?) to take some outdoor photos of us posing with our birds and looking all mean and moody in front of the graffiti covered council garages near the flats where I was living at the time. We chose what we all thought was the best photo to put on the front cover and found some old family album photos of me, Gary and Paul as young kids to put on the back of the record sleeve too.

A question I often get asked is who the women are posing with us on that iconic front cover? The women on that records sleeve are Anita, my then wife (sadly no longer with us), Paula, Gary's girlfriend and Gymslips guitarist as well as Paul's cousin Gill who's the punky looking one (a last minute replacement for the girlfriend Mandy who had dumped him just a few days before).

The music press, critics and fanzines gave us mixed reviews but on the whole I think most of them found something they liked on our debut album.

Garry Bushell's review in Sounds however was not a very favourable one at all. At that time I recall Gal's less than impressed comments saying something like he had been listening to a lot of Slade at the time and that we were not much in comparison. Well something like that anyway. Now I've never held it against him because Mister Bushell has always been a diamond geezer to us (and still continues to be) and is always very helpful and full of good advice. I was disappointed, at the time, of course because I thought it a bit unfair to compare us to Slade who are one of the most legendary skinhead bands of all time but it's a free country and he was of course entitled to his own opinion. To be fair he also did an interview with me and

Gary that made it into Sounds too which was really humorous and observant so I'm pretty proud of that. He also more recently (after I had reformed The Ejected) steered me towards Randale Records in Germany, when I asked for his advice about a new record deal so I do have plenty of positive things to say about him.

In the last forty odd years that have passed by I have often seen or been shown many horrible reviews of Ejected records and to be honest they're the ones that make me laugh. Something about the creative ways or descriptions to illustrate how much they loathe the band are actually quite hilarious. One guy described my vocals on a particular song as like I had 'climbed into a blender' to sing them and to be fair when I listened back to the particular Ejected song he was criticising he wasn't far wrong either.

Yet I have had so many positive things said to me about that 'A Touch Of Class' album from fans near and far. A lot of older punk fans that I've chatted to at gigs value it highly and I've had so many fans tell me that it is the sound of their punk teenage years. Ejected fans from America, Brazil, Sweden, Italy, France, Germany, Scotland and England often get in touch and say great things about my band which is always pleasing to hear.

One guy called Pete Gill who I met and chatted too at a recent gig down in Southampton told me that that our debut album had helped him get through his time at Feltham youth custody detention centre where he'd got banged up for a stretch in his late teens. He said every night after lights out all the inmates would start chanting the 'Oh Yeah, oh yeah' section of our song 'Carnival' so it echoed around the place. He also told me that 'A Touch Of Class' is one of his all-time favourite punk albums. I mean what a cool thing to hear from an old Ejected fan.

A Touch Of Class was out there back then and we were determined to try and do it justice by playing as many gigs as possible but there were a few problems with that.

We never did a tour.

We were basically confined to playing gigs in and around Essex and London.

The main reason for that was probably due to our domestic situations. We all had financial and family obligations and all three of us also held down full time jobs. Wives, girlfriends, bills, debts, rent, etc. Sounds weak I know but back in those days the only way to get on tour with the bigger, more well-known bands was to buy your way on the tour as the support band. Don't ask me why? None of us could afford to do that.

I do recall a phone conversation with Simon Edwards once about it when he said that Vice Squad were going out on a big UK tour and if we wanted to be their support act on that tour it would cost us two grand. Of course I suppose that we could have tried to raise the money but then how would we have afforded to buy a van, decent amps and gear to get us around? Let alone trying to persuade our work management to let us have the six weeks off work to go on tour whilst still be paying out our monthly rent and utility bills back home.

I suppose we could've tried to get bank or credit card loans out to pay for it all but in the end we just didn't do that. I believe deep down that we just couldn't risk all that we had for six weeks of travelling around the country and doing gigs against the risk of losing our homes and the comfortable way of life that we had gotten used to.

Sometimes I do wonder how things could have gone if I'd have forced the issue and gambled on getting the band a higher profile and expand our fan base.

Back then touring was the only accepted way of promoting your bands singles and albums. Maybe if we had gigged our way around the UK endlessly we might have had a hit single or boosted our album sales a bit. Not that we craved the big time really but it would have at least given us a bit of dosh to move the band upwards.

We were never big enough or lucky enough to sneak onto any television music shows like Top of the Pops, Whistle Test or any of the others. I must admit it was one aspect of being in a band that I had often fantasised about. An appearance on a mainstream TV music show could boost a bands record sales immensely back then but it never happened. We would often see bands like UK Subs, Sham 69, Undertones, Buzzcocks, Cockney Rejects, Rezillos, Damned and Siouxsie and the Banshees appearing on Top of the Pops and laugh about how we would look on the show doing '10p' or 'Fast 'n' Loud'.

Who knows what might have come from a TV appearance or two?

Maybe a bigger record label would've taken us on?

Who knows?

Also back then it was very hit or miss as to how good an Ejected gig would go.

Some were excellent, some were ordinary but a few were shambolic. Funny enough it's the really crap gigs that have stayed in my memory the longest.

We had plenty of excuses though. Our gear was cheap and nasty. We had crappy guitars and amps and a dodgy PA system that we hired for headline gigs (using an old hippy guy called Geoff) because he was cheap and reliable. Often we'd drink far too much to try and combat our stage nerves and sometimes end up so pissed we'd not know what songs we were playing. Fucking ridiculous right?

One awful gig we did at the Three Rabbits in Manor Park Gary and I were so pissed up that we stopped mid-song on stage because he was playing 'Mr Muggins' and I was playing 'Gang Warfare'. We then had a drunken row with each other on stage arguing about it. I remember looking up to see our audience walking out the doors in disgust and the venue manager behind the bar with his hands on his hips shaking his bald head and glaring at us. So we obviously didn't get paid that night as our whole performance had been a drunken mess.

Hilarious to recount nowadays but back then it signalled a big weakness in the band and the cracks were soon beginning to show.

Band rehearsals were not much better either.

We rehearsed at a place called Allen Gordons (it went on to be called Thunder Dome studios) which was located under the railway arches at Leyton Midland train station. It was good because it was fairly local and two of the four rehearsal rooms were kitted out with Marshall amplifier's (mounted on the wall and caged behind heavy duty mesh frames to dissuade theft), a PA system, microphones and a drum kit all included in the price of the room hire. So we didn't need to lug our own amps and drum kit along. We just took our guitars and plugged in and off we went.

Of course those huge Marshall amps made us sound more powerful as it beefed up my guitar sound and Gary's bass too but really we should have invested in some better amps ourselves to use at gigs, especially the ones where we were the headlining act.

Anyway once every few weeks we would book a block of eight hours rehearsal time in one of the kitted out rooms (between ten and six) and split the time into two blocks of four hours so that either Anita's band Ginger 'n' Spice or The Gymslips could share the rehearsal room time with us.

We would let the girls have the first four hours while the three of us would slope off down the road to the café for a greasy fry up and mug of tea. Then at around half eleven we'd saunter back up the road to the Three Blackbirds pub and sink five or six pints before heading back for our block of four hours rehearsal time at two.

Sometimes if the girl bands were still rehearsing we would go upstairs to the 'rec room' which had a pool table for bands that arrived early and were waiting around and play a few frames or we'd get distracted by the Space Invader and Pac Man arcade machines for an hour. Plus the two lovely old ladies that worked in reception would offer to make us big mugs of tea.

Eventually we would resign ourselves to maybe a couple of hours of actual rehearsing the songs but even then we'd keep stopping every so often for cigarette and toilet breaks.

On a couple of occasions we even had a sleep on the floor amongst our equipment because all the booze and greasy food had made us drowsy. Several times we'd get woken up by other bands knocking on the door just after six and asking if they could get in the room now?

Yet we'd laugh it off like we were a cool and well-rehearsed outfit. Pathetic I know but hilarious looking back at the band that were as full of apathy as they were anarchy.

This wasn't all the time of course. Usually I'd arrive at a band practise with maybe a couple of good song ideas and Gary usually had some lyrics too.

Funnily enough the best Ejected songs were written in like five or ten minutes I can remember writing both 'I'm Gonna Get A Gun' and 'Fast 'n' Loud' really quickly. To be honest I am still doing it like that today, well the initial guitar riff, song structure and lyrics. All the best ideas come quickly and sort of write themselves. So that is honestly how we were back then just unambitiously happy to be playing local gigs and getting drunk.

Chapter five

We were playing gigs and then we recorded our second EP titled 'Noise For The Boys' which we recorded at Pineapple studios over in Southall for some reason. It was famous for being the recording studio where Judie Tzuke had cut her successful single 'Stay With Me Till Dawn' which had gotten to number 16 in the UK charts. Southall was one of West London's first multi-cultural areas at that time, which we soon found out when between recording sessions we popped into a local pub near the studio to find a guy behind the bar wearing a turban. As we got served we looked around and realised that most of the punters in the bar were wearing turbans too which at that time was quite a rare sight for us East London lads.

The three songs we did were 'Fast 'n' Loud', 'I Don't Care' and 'What Happened In Brighton?' and we had a lot of fun recording them with a guy called Phil Chilton (who I think Simon Edwards hired to produce us). Anyway it came out sounding pretty good and again was well received by the music press, fanzines and our own growing fan base in and around the Dagenham area.

Now it was around this time The Gymslips were becoming quite popular, after throwing Anita out the band, because they had simplified their once melodic pop songs into a more punky street sound, which I always maintain The Ejected had influenced them. As we were always hanging around with them it probably made them realise that raw, simple punk songs were getting us noticed and so decided to adopt the same tactics. So the now three piece girl band started writing songs about everyday life with catchy choruses and shouty vocals. They dropped the schoolgirl uniform thing from their live act in favour of denim jeans, leather jackets and monkey boots and it was working for them. Writing and singing songs about pie and mash, binge drinking, sex, agony aunt columns, takeaway food and being 'Renes'(east end slang for geezer birds). They even got a session on the John Peel show followed by a record deal with Abstract Records and things were really starting to happen for them. Paula Richards was Gary's girlfriend and as he had a transit van she started asking him to be the bands driver stroke roadie and to drive them to the many gig offers they were now getting from all over the country.

So this then became a problem for us and consequently a dilemma for Gary too trying to negotiate the Ejected rehearsals or gigs to not clash with Gymslips stuff.

One day quite out of the blue Gary told me that he had decided to leave The Ejected as he wasn't enjoying it as much anymore. He also understandably wanted to spend more time with Paula as she toured around Britain with The Gymslips.

Part of me completely understood his reasons but the other part of me felt betrayed. I was angry and confused but in the end it was what he wanted to do and so I just had to accept it.

Obviously, me and drummer Paul wanted to carry on and so now we had to find a bass player to replace Gary which was not going to be easy. It was like losing my left arm. We had started The Ejected together and now he was leaving. So not only did I need to find a great bassist but it had to be someone who I liked and could get on with as well.

So along came Paul 'Bruna' Quain.

He was one of the first people to reply to the ad in Sounds classifieds and we auditioned him the following weekend at Scarf studios and he was a breath of fresh air. Not only an experienced bassist but was easy going, creative and a good laugh as well. After his successful audition in which he nailed all the bass lines to our songs we took him to the pub around the corner for a few beers and a chat.

All seemed good and we played a few great gigs with him at Feltham Football Club with Welsh punk rockers The Partisans as support. We also did a rare gig on our own doorstep at the Regency, in Chadwell Heath, which was really packed and sweaty and we ended up doing several encores.

We had a crew of local fans now that followed us around and things were looking up again.

Riot City said we could record a third single now as were a whole band again and so we recorded the 'Press The Button' EP at Scarf Studios in Bromley-By-Bow with three new songs called 'Russians', 'In The City' and '24 Years'.

Now that Gary had gone Paul Griffiths decided that he needed to help me out a bit on the song writing duties and would, every now and then, hand me scraps of paper with hastily written lyrics on them as possible new song ideas. 'Russians' turned out to be one of his better ones. Admittedly the lyrics he had written didn't seem to rhyme or scan very well but I felt both touched and grateful that he was at least attempting to contribute. I listened to how Paul sung the chorus of "I spy with my little eye, there goes another Russian spy, I spy eye to eye, where's your national pride.. oh yeah" and I really liked it. So with a quick rewrite to the verses and then coming up with a guitar riff to compliment the melody we managed to cobble together a pretty decent punk anthem. The Ejected fans really seem to love that song at gigs too. So it became the lead track of the new EP.

We had fun recording the new songs on the EP and our third single did okay.

Now around this time Anita became pregnant and she persuaded Barking & Dagenham council to let us move from her small one bedroom flat to a modest two bedroomed, terraced house not far away. So in July 1983, at the age of 24, I became a first time father, which added a lot of extra stress and responsibility into my life. I was still working five days a week as a warehouseman as well as doing all the band stuff.

So once my son Adam was born, we moved into the house and we now had a baby to contend with it meant that instead of Anita or I going off out to band rehearsals or to play gigs whenever we fancied it our life had now changed forever and that one or the other of us would need to look after the baby whilst we took turns in continuing in our respective bands. Anita had formed a new all girl rock band by this time called Minx and they were getting regular gig offers too.

Simon Edwards rang me shortly afterwards and asked me how I felt about the idea of The Ejected recording a second album? Also did we have enough new songs to put on a new record? I was so excited at the thought of going back into the recording studio again that I lied and said 'yeah, we have loads of new songs ready to go'.

Simon said okay and to send him a rough demo tape of the new songs to listen to and he would give them a listen himself to check out how good they were.

I came off of that phone call feeling elated but also panicked as we only had maybe four new songs in our set.

But around this time something really weird happened too.

Paul Quain disappeared.

I only had one phone number to contact Bruna on, which was at his bedsit in Elephant and Castle. Yet every time I rang it and asked to speak to him, his Asian landlord answered by telling me that he hadn't seen Bruna around for ages. He wasn't in his room even though all his stuff was all still there, so he hadn't done a bunk either. Over that week I kept on calling him but no luck and Bruna didn't call me back at all either. It was a mystery.

Was he dead? Had he gone abroad? Or was he pissed off at us for some unknown reason?

It was very frustrating.

And time was ticking.

I didn't know his address or anything and with this possible new album looming I had no choice but to ring Gary up and explain this problem to him and ask him, for old times sake, if he could possibly do the new album with us? As we couldn't rely on the elusive Mister Quain turning up on time.

Luckily Gary said yes, as The Gymslips were off the road for a few weeks, so that was a big relief. I thanked him but then told him about needing to write about seven or eight new songs in the next seven to ten days and that we would need to rehearse and tape them to send up to Simon at Riot City.

Several months after Spirit Of Rebellion came out, I got a phone call one evening and when I picked up a familiar male voice said, 'Hello Jim? It's me Paul Quain, listen I'm really sorry."

I was stunned to hear his voice after almost giving up on ever hearing from him again. He wanted to explain but did not want to do it on the phone. So we arranged to meet at my local pub later that evening.

The following is his account of the mysterious disappearance of Bruna Quain.

One day, several months ago, he and a few of his friends had been out to buy twelve tabs of acid. Bruna had them in his pocket as they walked home through dodgy South London.

A police van appeared from around the corner and swerved over towards them and a lot of cops started piling out to stop and search them all under the 'SUS law' that was very popular at that time.

Bruna had panicked. He couldn't throw the tabs of acid away in case the cops spotted him doing it so instead he impulsively swallowed them. All twelve tabs, thinking that once the Old Bill had finished searching them all and found nothing and fucked off, he could then stick his fingers down his throat and puke up the drugs before they had been ingested properly.

But guess what?

Unfortunately a couple of his mates were carrying some weed and they were all told to get in the back of the meat wagon and so he had no chance to vomit up the evidence. Bruna then went on the biggest hallucinatory trip of his life.

Long story short he went mad and so consequently after the police let him go was sectioned for three months in a mental health facility until he calmed down. Even then the paranoia and fear that acid induces had stayed with him. He was trying to get his life back on track but it wasn't easy.

He had lost his bedsit room and all his belongings too including his bass guitar and amplifiers. He had to go and explain to the dole office where he had been for three months and that he was now living back with his parents.

I sat in shock and disbelief as he told me his story. I had been expecting some bullshit excuses but this was next level crazy and totally skewed. I could tell it was the truth though because the Paul Quain I'd briefly known was a funny, confident, chatty and cool dude. The Paul Quain that sat in front of me that night was as twitchy as fuck, emaciated, pale faced and just a bit paranoid. He also kept glancing nervously behind him every time the pub door opened. He went on to tell me that even now months later if he went into a shop and asked for a loaf of bread and they asked him what type of bread, he'd just get suddenly freaked out and leave. He was a broken shell of a man. I felt so sorry for him and then had to break the news to him that he had missed recording a brand new Ejected album with legendary UK Subs guitarist Nicky Garratt as producer. He was gutted. Most of all he was so apologetic like he had let us all down.

A sad story.

A sort of funny one though and a lesson for all you druggies and junkies out there too.

We said our farewells outside The Admiral Vernon pub in Broad Street, Dagenham at closing time we vowed to stay in touch but I never saw or spoke to him ever again. Shame because he really was a top bloke and a great bass player.

Chapter six

It has been almost forty years since the recording of the 'Spirit Of Rebellion' album. Yet I can remember the frantic weeks of desperate preparation leading up to it quite well.

Simon Edwards was based up in Bristol so he had no idea of how many songs we had in our set. So this made it easier for me to lie to him about having lots of new punk anthems for a second Ejected album.

After the phone conversation I'd had with him about doing a second album and having plenty of songs to put on it I just remember panicking and sitting down on the floor of the lounge with my guitar, a notepad and pen everyday and watching the TV news or reading newspapers and magazines looking for lyrical inspiration.

Within about five days I had written the songs 'Afghan Rebels', 'War Cry', 'Greenham Woman', 'Army Song', 'Dirty Schoolgirls' ' Young Punks, Go For It' and 'Mental Case'. Gary had managed to come up with a fast punk song called 'Hang 'Em High' and a reggae number called 'Stop, Look And Listen'.

So at the next rehearsal we practised all these new songs relentlessly, along with our version of the Stranglers classic 'Go Buddy Go'. Paul had even had a go at writing the lyrics of a song about his ex-girlfriend who had famously dumped him before the A Touch Of Class photo shoot and who was now (according to him) putting it about a bit and shagging all of his mates. After I revamped Paul's rather vindictive lyrics a bit and sorted out a guitar riff for it we eventually turned it into 'Mary Go Round', which although not a punk rock classic, is (in my opinion) a pretty good song in its own right I reckon. I persuaded him to swap Mandy to Mary so as to avoid any future litigation issues. Anyway 'Mary-Go-Round' sounded better.

Also around this time I had also recruited a mate and work colleague called Kevin Pallet to the band .He played lead guitar pretty well and he performed in a pub and club covers band at weekends. Really boring stuff too because I had gone along to watch him play one night and they did stuff like The Eagles 'Lying Eyes', Dire Straits 'Romeo And Juliet' and Bruce Springsteen's 'Born To Run' YAWN!

Yet Kev was a funny guy and we got on great at work and The Ejected really needed a lead guitarist to bolster up our sound.

It was my attempt to solve the ongoing problem of us not having guitar solos in our songs. As I have said previously I'm a half decent rhythm guitarist but I cannot play a lead solo to save my life.

So I asked Kev to join us even though Punk and Oi music wasn't his thing. He did however like the idea of playing on an album and I think that is what persuaded him in the end.

I introduced him to Paul and Gary at a band practise and they all got on great.

We had to teach him how to play punk guitar though. Kev owned a Fender Stratocaster so that wasn't ideal. We would often have to stop him during a guitar solo because he'd be off trying to emulate an Eric Clapton or a Mark Knophler style solo. Basically we had to knock that shit out of him quick. I'd patiently hum how I thought the guitar solo should go in each song and he'd find the notes until he finally sussed it and copied it on the fretboard. We also gave him the rehearsal tapes to take home to try and learn off by heart.

And so eventually I posted off a cassette tape of the new material to Simon at Riot City and then anxiously waited.

So by the time Simon got back to me we were a four piece outfit and he had listened to the new songs and told me that he really loved the new stuff. PHEW!

There was a BUT though. He didn't want us to produce the new album. A Touch Of Class had a rough and raw sound to it which was mostly down to our inexperienced yet enthusiastic production and mixing technique.

Simon's main concern about us doing a second album was the production side of it, he wanted a more polished and professional sound. He then asked me if I could think of anyone in the same punk genre who I admired and that might possibly work with us to produce the new record.

Two names instantly sprang to mind: Micky Geggus, the guitarist of The Cockney Rejects or Nicky Garratt my guitar and song writing hero from the UK Subs both of whom had production credits under their belts too.

Simon said he'd look into it and get back to me. I was now very fucking excited.

So when Simon did get back to me a few days later to tell me that he had talked with Nicky Garratt and that Nicky had actually heard of The Ejected and was showing interest I nearly fainted. Apparently Nicky had requested a copy of our first album and our three singles to listen to before making his decision.

I was almost in Punk Heaven.

But again I had to wait.

The call finally came about a week later and it was fantastic news. Nicky Garratt had liked our records but he insisted on coming along to see us play at our next band rehearsal to observe and take notes.

Gary and Paul were also UK Subs fans so we were all very excited and psyched too. Except for Kev, who said "The UK who…?"

So it was quickly arranged that Nicky would attend our next Saturday morning rehearsal. I was sick with anxiety and nerves. To meet one of you idols is one thing but to possibly work with one was just fucking mind blowing. Not to mention a once in a lifetime opportunity.

Here's a really weird, fortuitous, ironic and flabbergasting twist of fate though.

Nicky Garratt was living in Bromley-By-Bow in a tower block not five hundred yards away from Scarf Studios where we recorded 'A Touch Of Class' and sometimes rehearsed. I shit you not!

So he was living just ten tube stops away from Dagenham. What were the odds? The guy is from Blackburn, had been all around the world with The UK Subs and yet there he was living in East London the home of The Ejected.

It seemed like fate.

So come that Saturday morning pulling up to Dagenham East station, where we had arranged to pick Nicky up from, I was more nervous than I had been on my wedding day and at the birth of my son all rolled together.

And there was a bearded guy in a black anorak holding a guitar case looking nothing like the bleached, blonde, spiky haired, bare chinned, young guitarist from out of the UK Subs.

We were a bit confused and then laughed as I rolled down the side window and I actually asked him "Are you Nicky Garratt? What a dick!

He nodded and climbed into the van and seemed a bit nervous and very quiet.

Now, in hindsight, the experience of meeting four young and excited punk rockers out in the wilds of Dagenham probably had him a bit anxious and nervous too.

I remember Nicky just standing over by a wall in the rehearsal room we'd booked at a Dagenham studio that we had just started using (that Kev had told us about) watching us and not saying very much. As we set up our gear I warned him that our new songs were still a bit rough and ready but he just said not to worry about it and to just play them. So we played all the new songs while he watched and listened and remained quiet. I remember we fucked up quite a bit partly due to nerves but mostly out of still not knowing the songs that well yet. We kept apologising to him and Kev's guitar solos were 'extra cringe' and I honestly thought we'd fucked our chances.

After an hour or so of bumbling our way through the new material Nicky suggested we do some of our old songs for him and we steamed through those easily and I remember Nicky looking a lot happier. Like he had thought 'oh right, these boys can play good after all'.

When we finally downed instruments for a much needed smoke and tea break I took the opportunity to ask him to be honest with us.

He was smiling and told us that we seemed like a good bunch of genuine guys and he actually liked that the new songs weren't set in stone yet. He said there was plenty of room for his help and input. He wanted a challenge. Apparently the last band he'd produced an album with had all their songs down pat and he had found the sessions boring. So ironically our lazy, slapdash approach had actually worked in our favour and secured us Nicky Garratt's services.

Nicky said he had some decent gear of his own that he would bring over to the recording studio which would improve our overall sound.

After we dropped him back at the tube station and said our goodbye's everybody was well excited. It was like this was going to be the launch pad for The Ejected to finally take off.

Nicky called up Simon to confirm that he'd do it and then Simon rang me. I'll always remember that phone call because Simon, who was usually so upbeat and happy, sounded a bit anxious and annoyed.

"Don't fuck this up okay because I'm paying Nicky a lot more than I had expected to do on this album production. So I will be coming down this time to the studio to check on you guys and make sure you don't waste precious studio time or fuck about," he said (or something very similar). His tone took the wind out of my sails a bit but not for long though because I was going to be working with Nicky Garratt the best punk guitarist ever!

Chapter seven

Working on Spirit Of Rebellion turned out to be a lot harder work than any of us had expected.

At first I was in awe, recording an album with legendary, UK Subs axe man Nicky Garratt. The co-writer of such punk classics as 'CID', 'Stranglehold', 'Tomorrows Girls', 'Warhead' and 'Emotional Blackmail'.

I needn't have worried because he was such a kind and generous bloke.

After seeing the crappy 'SG' copy guitar and 30 watt combo amp that I had been using I think he took pity on me because when we turned up at Scarf studios for the very first recording session, he had a surprise for me. Nicky had brought along his very own Marshall stack and his personal Gordon Smith 'Black Shadow' guitar for me to use, plus a Fender Strat for Kev to use.

The Marshall amp-head and speaker cab even had the UK Subs logo stencilled onto them as they had most likely been around the world a few times and been with him everywhere. His guitar had been customised by Gordon Smith for him as he preferred it in black so they had obliged and named it 'Black Shadow' in his honour. It made that definitive crunchy, raw Subs style rhythm guitar sound that I loved so much. The album sounds stronger for it too thanks to Nicky's generous nature.

Nick's generosity spread to helping us out with the new songs too which, in my opinion, taking our basic two dimensional offerings and giving them an overhauling into three dimensional songs.

The eerie background vocals and shouts on 'Afghan Rebels' for instance were his idea. Sceptical at first at what he meant, we tried it out but were not really sure what he was trying to achieve but once he played back the track to us afterwards with the extra backing vocals added we were stunned by the result and impressed with Nicky's creative vision.

The vocal effect on 'Mental Case' was his idea too that made my voice sound slightly disembodied and evil almost like I could actually be singing that song from inside a padded cell. He just gave my microphone tons of reverb apparently and pushed it through some parabolic gizmo on the mixing desk.

Nicky was striving to make each song different and to give each track its own individual personality. If 'A Touch Of Class' was a rollercoaster ride of speedy, raw edged, singalong terrace anthems then this album was going to be a more polished affair with added depth and more instrument awareness.

Nicky Garratt was like a 'Mad Scientist' trying to perfect the 'Monster' that was The Ejected. Whenever Kev struggled with a solo or a lead fill Nick would try and help him out but often it was both easier and time saving for Nicky to play the lead fills or solo's rather than spending valuable studio time trying to show Kev how it should go. Nicky wasn't flash or condescending about it either and never put Kev's nose out of joint.

That big slash of a 'G' chord in the intro riff to 'Army Song' was Nicky's clever idea too (another simple example of elevating a good song and making it better) he also added the repetitive guitar lead hook line and even played the solo in the middle of that track because Kev was struggling with it.

The dub section in the middle of 'Greenham Woman' was another case in point. Whenever I listen to that Ejected reggae track now it still seems so effortless and cool, yet Nicky laboured over the dub section for a good six or seven hours at least trying to get it just how he liked it. We all got so bored of hearing it being perfected over and over that we pissed off down the chip shop and then into the local pub and let him get on with it. We could be fickle bastards back then but when we eventually returned to the studio and listened to his final mix of it we were blown away.

Despite all this Nicky was a funny guy and easy to get on with and as the days rolled by we got to know him a bit better and he got to suss us out too.

Most of the final decisions within the band were taken by me. The songs that were given the thumbs up, the artwork for the singles and albums, the gig finding and booking, publicity, interviews and photos were all in my domain. Yet here in the studio with Nicky in charge it soon became a running joke between us all about who had the final say about the final mix of each track, overdubs, vocal additions and what guitar solos to leave in or out. Gary, Kev and Paul seemed quite happy to take a back seat but I always had an opinion and often battled with Nicky for the final word.

Nicky commented that "The Ejected was a democracy run by a fascist dictator."

It was funny because it was true. It had just never been spoken aloud before. All of the Ejected songs were my babies but Nicky was just trying to help them grow up a bit.

The Smiths were becoming popular at that time but I just couldn't stand them (and still fucking can't) what with the meandering, jangly guitars and Morrissey's annoying, whimpering vocal style. It seemed to me that they were the opposite of everything that The Ejected stood for.

Nicky loved The Smiths with a passion and kept trying to convince me how ground breaking they were (I acknowledge that fact now but still sort of despise them). We spent hours good naturedly debating the merits of their growing popularity but I was never going to concede and neither was Nicky.

Yet I loved being in the studio environment with Nicky and there was rarely a dull moment apart from the afternoon we recorded 'The Enemy Awaits' track.

This was a song that Nicky wrote and recorded with the UK Subs but was very unhappy about how it eventually sounded and asked us if we would do a version for the album. Of course this was immensely flattering to us, our punk rock hero asking little old us to improve on one of his own self-penned songs so we got very excited and said yes. Anyway Nick played us the Subs version which was okay and then sorted out the lyrics and chords for us to quickly learn.

We told Nicky that at gigs we sometimes played a Subs cover for an encore in the early days as we didn't have many songs back then so would churn out our own versions of 'Tomorrows Girls', 'Killer' or 'CID'.

The Enemy Awaits is a slow, brooding song loaded with menace and has a heavy grinding atmosphere to it. We all agreed it would fit on the new album great.

The trouble was it was Nicky's baby and boy did he take control of it. I can remember playing and recording the guitar riff over and over, take after take until Nicky seemed satisfied and then he did the same with Paul's drumming and Gary's bass. He seemed so seriously driven to get it just so. We had no wiggle room to do it our way at all. I remember attempting the lead vocal and he was on my case all the time. Take after excruciating take as he never seemed satisfied. However I sang it just wasn't exactly right. I even asked Gary to have a go because I was getting so pissed off with it but he struggled with it even worse, trying and failing to do each vocal inflection exactly how Nicky wanted it. So back into the vocal booth I went once more, doing each verse, phrase by bastard phrase and word by fucking word with Nicky listening back to each take analysing and replaying it a zillion times. He sucked all the pleasure and enjoyment out of it for us. Eventually, many hours later, he finally seemed satisfied with the end result and the fans, music critics and album reviewers seemed to like it too.

But they weren't there GRRR!

I can't listen to it anymore because it is just a reminder of that torturous session and how Nicky Garratt somehow reduced the excitement of recording a song down to unenjoyable hard work.

Did I mention that Nicky had left the Subs by this time?

Apparently after almost ten years, he'd finally had enough of the endless grind of gigging and the repetitive nature of writing songs, recording and touring only to rinse and repeat.

Apart from that Nicky had no regrets but felt that he needed to leave the band and to do other things but was very proud of his time with the Subs.

Nicky was full of great Subs stories too, telling us tales of his time in the band and all his many adventures on the road over the years.

After recording at the studio would be finished for the day we would often go back with him up to the high rise flat that he shared with a girl called Rebecca for a drink and sit chatting for an hour or two before going home. Nick explained to us that he was in a transitional period of his life and was busy making plans to move out to the USA to live, record and explore a new chapter of his life. So we realised that we'd been lucky to get him too. A few months later and he'd have been gone. He sold me his Marshall amp-head cheap and gave us all a few bits of Subs memorabilia too before he went off to the States.

Nicky was a kind, generous, funny, charismatic, gentle and interesting guy and probably still is.

I look back on that time with fondness and pride. I think he is based in San Francisco these days and I am truly grateful to him for that fantastic experience back then.

Before he did go Simon hired him again for us to record a fourth single (which due to unforeseen circumstances never got released by Riot City Records).

I had written a new song called 'Public Animal Number 1' and hastily penned a rough B-side called 'Skinheads On The Street'. We had also been working on a cover version of Alice Cooper's 'Generation Landslide' to put on it as well.

During those few days of recording Nicky's female flat mate Rebecca came along with him as she was a budding vocalist herself. She was skinny, blonde, attractive, outgoing and very flirty too. She asked me if she could be on one of the songs in any way (probably fluttering her eyelashes at me with a hand on my thigh too) and so I suddenly thought up a genius idea for a punk rock duet song.

I stepped out of the studio and hastily re-wrote the lyrics to the 'Skinheads On The Street' song but keeping the riff of the song and came up with 'Rock Star' a duet for Rebecca and me to sing. We had great fun singing and recording that duet too about a punk rocker bragging to a female fan about how famous he would be one day and she wisely doubting his every word. Even nowadays it still makes me laugh when I hear it and reckon if it had been released as a single it might well have troubled the UK charts even?

All three tracks can be found on either the best of album (that Captain Oi released a few years later) and on the CD re-release of 'Spirit Of Rebellion'.

Spirit Of Rebellion didn't sell too well upon release and shortly after that Riot City Records folded and The Ejected decided to stop too. Punk rock was pushed back into the shadows by the mid 80's pop revolution and so eventually we decided to call it a day.

Dawn Patrol gig at Walthamstow Youth Centre 1980

The New Hawaiians with Jim, Gary, Paul & Kev

Gary, Paul and Big Jim pose for press 1982

What a poseur in his bedroom 1980

Live at Regency Suite Chadwell Heath. Paul Quain, Big Jim, Paul Griffiths & Dynamo Kev

Gary, Paula, Jim, Anita, Sarah & Paul posing for album cover

The Ejected's three Eps (artwork by Jim)

Class of '82

45

The Ejected at Rebellion Festival 2014. Paul, Danny, Jim & Jonny

Jim & Paul with Charlie Harper at The Fleece, Bristol 5.5.17

The Ejected new line up – Jim, Paul, Jonny & Toby

Jim Brooks - Vocals

Jonny Romain - Guitar

Paul Berry - Bass

Toby Thacker - Drums

Chapter eight

"So Jim," I hear you cry, "what the fuck were you doing for thirty years before reforming the Ejected again in 2014?"

Good question!

The Ejected had finished when Riot City went under in 1984 and Punk and Oi music was apparently on the way out, plus gigs were getting harder to come by for bands like us.

It was time to do something different.

I'd always been a fan of reggae and dub music and so had Gary. UB40 had been our favourites all along and they had steadily gotten more and more popular at this time and they were becoming regulars in the UK top 40 and album charts.

So we thought we'd have a go.

For a while Paul, Gary, Kev and I formed a pop/reggae band called The New Hawaiians. We recruited a saxophonist (Eric), a keyboardist (Dave) and two girl singers (Tracy and Karen) and we started to write our own reggae songs. We had enjoyed the few reggae style Ejected songs that we had written and recorded on both Ejected albums and realised that we had a certain flair for playing pop reggae and soon we had a strong set list of original reggae songs plus a few covers thrown in. So before we knew it we got a couple of gig offers too. The first was an outdoor charity bash in Debden, Essex. We all donned Hawaiian shirts for the gig as a sort of jokey gimmick for the new band. Fortunately we went down quite well. The second gig we played was a few weeks later at the Rock Garden as support to The Gymslips. The Rock Garden crowd also seemed to really enjoy our new danceable brand of pop/reggae music too and things seemed to be looking up once more.

Until a few months later when, out of the blue, Gary and Paul suddenly announced that they were leaving the band to do their own thing and took one of the female singers (Karen, who Gary was knocking off at the time after he had split up with Paula from The Gymslips) with them to form a band called 4 Minutes To Moscow.

So, I was back to square one again and not wanting to give up on a good thing I decided to replace them firstly with Mick Robinson on drums plus I still had Kev with me and Eric our sax player. Also Dave the keyboard guy was in too. Through the music papers classifieds, I found a great mixed-race guy called Chas Mark from Hackney who played reggae bass superbly and a couple of black girl singers called Lorna and Vanessa who auditioned well. And so, with this great new line up I renamed the band Jo Jo Republic and we recorded a great demo tape with songs called 'Run Johnny Run', 'Love Games' and a reggae-fied cover of 'First Cut Is The Deepest', the old PP Arnold song.

This was around 1986/87 and I had just gotten divorced from Anita and was living in a bedsit in Rush Green, Romford.

Keeping a few of the New Hawaiian's songs whilst adding a lot of new ones that I had been writing, we soon had an even stronger set of very catchy pop/reggae songs especially with the addition of the two talented girl singers. Lead vocal duties were now shared between me, Kev and Lorna as and when each song required it. Slower more melodic numbers were for Lorna's sweet voice whilst Kev and I dealt with the up tempo songs. Mick Robinson's drumming was tight with Chas's throbbing, pulsating bass runs and Eric shared solo sax duties with Kev's lead guitar. I stuck to rhythm guitar and sung lead vocals on maybe six of our twelve best songs.

I still have the demo tapes and a couple of live sets on cassette and those songs still sound (in my humble opinion) as vibrant and valid today as they did back then.

We played a few local clubs and gradually began to build up a small following of fans. We quite often played at The Tunnel Club, south of the river and would get the whole place buzzing. It was a totally different vibe from my Ejected days but it was still a great feeling seeing the audience singing and dancing along to our songs.

I also managed to wangle a meeting with a music promotions company in Beckenham (incidentally, just up the road from that council estate I had grown up on as a kid that I told you about in Chapter One) in Kent. They had really loved our demo tape which I'd sent to them and were also hearing good feedback about us. At that time they had Brilliant on their books who's single 'It's A Man's, Man's, Man's World' was moving up the UK singles chart steadily and, I believe, Youth from Killing Joke was behind that single.

I attended that meeting and all went well. The two guys really liked the fact that our songs were original and that I was the writer too. I took along a live tape for them to listen to that also impressed them. So it was decided that we were to do a showcase at a prestige south London night club for them just so they could see for themselves how good a live act we were. They gave me a date and time and I went away happy thinking that here I was yet again on the brink of possibly getting another record deal for us.

Unfortunately the other seven members could not agree to the time and date specified for the showcase due to several of them having unavoidable work or family commitments that they could not get out of. So I managed to get the promotions company to reschedule the showcase and told the band how significant this showcase could be for us and how crucial it was that we not fuck these guys around. Yet once again several of the band members said they couldn't do the rescheduled date either. I remember ringing each one up individually and begging, cajoling and insisting that they change their plans for this possibly life changing audition. Yet it just wasn't happening and the level of band commitment seemed to have suddenly dropped away for some reason and all my efforts were falling on deaf ears. So our big opportunity passed, along with any hope of a possible record deal too. This rare and precious chance was just thrown away.

So, angry, frustrated and disappointed I just gave up.

I reluctantly hung up my guitar and started to sort my own life out. I met my second wife Carmel and we eventually got a council flat together and we got married in 1993 and I forgot about playing in bands and making music for a while to concentrate on work, home life and buying a house. I became a father for the second time (with a daughter Keely in 1998) and settled down like everyone else to a life of full time work, paying the bills, mortgage and family stuff.

In 1999 Captain Oi Records run by Mark Brennan (ex-Business band member) contacted me about re-releasing both Ejected albums on CD and he also asked me to compile a 'best of' album that he would also put out.

He also asked if I could get the band to reform and record some new songs as bonus tracks for inclusion on the 'best of' album saying that he would cover all the recording costs. It sounded good to me.

I contacted both Gary and Kev who were both up for it as they were not in bands any more either but I had lost touch with Paul Griffiths the drummer and so had Gary and Kev. So I quickly wrote a couple of new punk songs called 'Road Rage', 'I Think I Just Saw Elvis' and Gary wrote some lyrics to a song that I put a guitar riff to called 'Violence Breeds Violence' and we revamped an old long forgotten Ejected song called 'Factory song'. We also did a rollicking cover version of 'All My loving' the old Beatles classic, as Mark Brennan told me that he was also planning to put out a compilation album containing punk versions of Beatles songs by lots of different Punk and Oi bands (which never happened if you were wondering?).

We went into a small recording studio in Upminster and used a Roland drum machine to replace Paul. I sent the finished songs to Mark over at Captain Oi and he put them on our 'best of' album.

Between 2000 and 2012, I did write and record a couple of England football songs before each of the major Euro and World Cup international cup tournaments and tried to find a record company to release them but with zero success. I wrote a song called 'Red Cross, White Flag' which is an absolute catchy, foot stomping banger, which did get played on an Essex local radio station called Time FM a few times but it never took off. I really should get 'Red Cross, White Flag' on an Ejected record in the future as I think it is a classic that needs to be heard.

I got divorced again in 2001 and ended up back on my own in a flat in Dagenham and had a string of failed relationships and jobs until I met my current girlfriend Kat, in 2013, at a new warehouse job that I started in March 2014. After telling her all about my old punk band she Googled my old Ejected band out of curiosity and interest one Saturday morning just to see how popular we had been. I had not really taken much notice of social media or what was going on with the internet explosion online thing. I owned a second hand laptop but only used it for trying to writing novels and sitcoms. Usually starting one but after fifty pages or so running out of enthusiasm due to a busy life working or tiredness and so on, so I never actually finished a novel.

    Anyway Kat was interested in my old band and as she scrolled through online sites she suddenly came across a recent message from some guy asking if anyone knew how to contact or get hold of Jim Brooks from the punk band The Ejected?

    Kat was intrigued and clicked on the message from the guy called Sean Hudson in Blackpool, who'd been visiting various pubs in Dagenham that had been name checked by me on the record sleeves of our singles and albums (The Three Travellers and The Eastbrook) and asking after me. I remember commenting that this guy sounded like a weirdo nutcase or a stalker, but Kat wanted me to message him back to find out what it was he wanted? So I replied to his message, saying I'm Jim Brooks why are you trying to contact me?

Chapter nine

Sean Hudson turned out to be a genuine Ejected fan and one time band and music promoter. He used to run the infamous Army & Navy pub and music venue in Chelmsford, Essex back in the day but had since relocated up to Blackpool and had started his own music merchandise and memorabilia business. He was also, quite surprisingly, the ex-husband of an old female friend of mine from back in the eighties.

I guess like many people, he'd been wondering what had happened to The Ejected and why one of the finest Punk and Oi bands from the early eighties was not still gigging or releasing stuff anymore?

So I rang Sean up to ask why he had been looking for me.

Sure enough he told me that he was a big Ejected fan and was wondering if I'd ever considered reforming the band again as the retro-punk gigging thing was now big once more? My first reaction was to tell him that I was probably too old for all that shit now, surely? I was fifty six at the time.

Sean explained that if I could somehow reform The Ejected that there would be decent money paid by promoters to see a band that was still highly regarded yet hadn't been seen 'live' in thirty years. Specifically he could get us on the bill at Rebellion Festival for that coming August and that he'd negotiate a good fee for us.

Rebellion (as a lot of you probably know) is one of the biggest annual gatherings of Punk, Oi, Indie and New Wave bands, old and new, in the UK and is held at the Winter Gardens in Blackpool on the first weekend in August each year.

Sean also told me that there was a big money offer from an American promoter of TNT festival over in Hartford, Connecticut for the end of September too (all flights and accommodation paid for) which seemed like a fantastic offer.

I told him that I'd think about it and get back to him.

I remember feeling quite flattered that people still cared about The Ejected after all this time and that we still had many fans young and old around the globe wanting to see us perform again.

To be honest my life had not been too exciting over the years after a string of failed relationships, falling out with friends, crappy, low paid warehouse jobs and the constant debt that had kept my spirits and expectations very low.

Kat said that I should definitely consider it and asked me if I knew where any of the other band members were and if they would perhaps be interested?

Truth was I'd fallen out with Gary ten years earlier and we had not spoken since and he really wouldn't want to be doing the whole 'retro punk thing' again anyway. The last I'd heard about Paul Griffiths was he'd married, had a kid and had moved away. I had no idea where to or if he still played drums anymore.

I did however have one friend who might be interested.

Paul Berry.

A young, ex-work colleague of mine who I'd worked alongside at a previous job for two years. He was a bass player and a good all round musician. He played in a couple of local bands at the time and I'd even dropped him off at band practices once or twice after work. We got on well (despite the thirty year age gap) and he had always shown an interest in my punk rock history and he'd even checked out The Ejected on YouTube and Google and on some other music streaming services. I also knew, from some of the crazy gig stories Paul had told me about that he knew and had played in bands with a wild drummer called Danny Blair who he had described to me as both brilliant and crazy.

So I messaged Paul and asked him to call me when he had a free moment.

Later that afternoon Paul called me and asked what was up? It had been about a year since I'd last seen or spoken to him. I quickly explained Sean Hudson's offer highlighting the prestigious and lucrative Rebellion Punk Festival and American TNT Festival offers for August and September and asked if he would be at all interested? Punk rock is not everyone's cup of tea but not only was Paul definitely interested he sounded quite enthusiastic too. He said that he would definitely be up for giving it a go and thought that his drummer mate, Danny would be too. Paul also added that he knew just the right guitarist friend of his to help out as well.

He said that he would find out for definite and then get back to me.

After that phone call ended I was hopeful but also reticent. Enthusiasm is one thing but recreating the old Ejected songs is totally another.

Paul rang me a couple of days later and said that not only were Danny and Jonny (the guitarist mate of his) interested but they had already met up at a rehearsal studio and they had run through and digitally recorded four or five Ejected songs (minus the vocals of course) and wanted to send those recordings to my mobile phone for me to listen to but I informed him that my mobile phone was a cheap Android piece of shit and that I probably wouldn't be able to access them. So Paul, being a bit of a tech nerd (or wizard if you prefer?) sent the digital recordings over to Kat's laptop by email so that we could listen and judge for ourselves.

When Kat opened up the email and pressed play I was instantly blown away.

The guitar, bass and drums were really explosive, gritty and raw.

The three young lads had not only emulated the Ejected sound and songs but had breathed new fire into them. I rang Paul straight back after listening to all five songs and told him to arrange us a proper band practise. I really needed to go and meet these guys.

So I contacted Sean Hudson just to keep him updated on the possibility that I might have reformed The Ejected, so long as my voice and bottle were still up to it and he sounded excited and pleased but I told him to hang fire for the moment as I still might not get on with these young guys or they might not like me, also that my vocals might be crap and did I still have the balls to walk out on a stage again and not fuck it up a second time around?

I also had to try and re-learn and remember all the lyrics to about twenty Ejected songs, after thirty years of not performing them, within a few days.

I turned up to a local rehearsal studio complex down the road from me in the wilds of Upminster called The Farm feeling very nervous.

Nerves are a good thing though because it means you care. I took plenty of beer and cigarettes along with me to ease myself in.

I needn't have worried because the guys were great.

Paul introduced me to Danny Blair and Jonny Romain and we all had a good time getting to know each other whilst chatting, laughing, drinking beer and smoking outside the big rehearsal room before getting started.

The guys were all younger than my son Adam and yet they didn't make me feel ancient or seem past it, in fact, they did quite the opposite in telling me quite genuinely how good they had found The Ejected's songs to be and how enjoyable it was to let rip on some raw, aggressive, fast, loud and infectiously catchy punk anthems. The bands that they were playing in around that time were boring pub covers bands or noodling, indie pop, type bands.

So into the rehearsal room we went and I got up on the low stage and tested out the microphone and gave each one of them a set list of the twenty songs and the running order I thought best for our debut.

We then proceeded to storm through the songs and it went very well. I was surprised at how loud and strong my voice still was after all the years and at how good it felt to be up there on stage.

Jonny's a very accomplished axe man and he does it all with consummate ease too including the raw rhythm guitar and the lead fills and solo's too. Danny was a powerhouse drummer and one of the best drummers I've ever played with (he took notes too, during and after each song which is unheard of and also showed great dedication). Paul's bass playing and sound was solid and formidable. They all seemed to be aware of the true essence of punk and get what it was about attitude, loudness, aggression-wise but also sticking to that good old Ejected sound. After all it would be the fans shelling out for tickets to see us, so it was only fair that we give those fans what it was they were paying for right?

So that was the new Ejected line up sorted out.

We agreed to do the Rebellion gig in Blackpool and Sean sounded well chuffed. He also told me to go check out the Ejected Facebook page. I wasn't even aware that there was an Ejected Facebook page. As I have said before up until that point I had very little to do with social media or online stuff, so I was gobsmacked when I saw literally hundreds of hits and comments from Ejected fans, old and new, from all around Europe and the USA. I was filled with disbelief and pride.

Why the fuck hadn't I done this ten years ago?

This gave me the extra resolve to make the new Ejected genuine. If the fans love us then the very least we owe them is a real Ejected experience. Not to be some covers band plodding wearily through just for a pay check. We were going to bring back the memories and try and create new ones too. So over the intervening period we rehearsed like mad and I even wrote a couple of new songs with the boys to try out and to include in our live set. The good ones survived but the rest have fallen by the wayside because Ejected songs must be the best that they can be. So at that time we wrote new songs like 'Dead Man Walking', 'Cops Are Coming' 'Zombie Girlfriend' and 'Attack, Attack, Attack' all of which made our live set and have been quite popular at our gigs ever since.

The Rebellion gig went well considering it was our very first proper gig. I sunk a few beers before going on that my son Adam had gone out and bought and I was feeling really nervous.

We hit that Blackpool stage and blasted through 'What Am I Gonna Do', 'East End Kids' and 'What Happened In Brighton?' and the crowd went wild. We were playing the Arena stage to about five hundred people. I was so relieved. The sound was great and the amps and drum kit loud. I relaxed a little and started to enjoy it a bit. The forty minutes flew by in a flash and before I knew it we were finishing with 'Have You Got 10p?' and I was sweaty, physically exhausted and mentally shagged out. Jonny's fingers were bleeding and Danny was grinning from ear to ear. Paul was sweaty and elated. Afterwards we went out to mingle with the crowd and find Sean Hudson. I shook so many fans hands and posed for selfies with them and even got asked to autograph stuff for them. I felt like a star but at the same time I was absolutely fucked.

It was a great first gig.

The Ejected were finally back.

We have played Rebellion three times all together (2014, 2016 and 2019) so far and each time has been great. I love that whole week leading up to the gig visiting the famous Tower Ballroom, Piers, pubs and everything surrounded by colourful punk characters.

Meeting up with friends and fans and drinking, chatting and smoking fags outside and getting recognised. Then there is always that obligatory someone who shouts out to me 'Oi, Jim, have you got 10p?' and I call back 'Nah, not me.' and then I realise that the Ejected are one of those bands who most punks know from that one famous and legendary song. It makes me smile and I find it kind of funny how I get recognised almost everywhere I go except in London and in Essex where I have fucking lived most of my life.

The second gig less than a month later was out in America in Hartford, Connecticut. We all flew out from Heathrow on American Airlines and felt like stars because it was all paid for. We got put up in a decent motel for three days and I got very drunk indeed. We headlined the festival on the Sunday night and did that yank crowd love us or what? They cheered, sung, stage dived and tried to take over the small stage and grab the microphone from me too. Check it out on YouTube because Kat filmed most of the songs from the side of a very chaotic and boisterous audience. We played faster and with more swagger and confidence this time and went down a storm. I really could not believe how many fans knew so many of the Ejected songs. They sang along to 'I'm Gonna Get A Gun', 'Army Song' and 'Young Tribes Of England' as well as 'Have You Got 10p?' and I was an absolute sweaty, wreck when we eventually came off of that stage. Yet still I had to sign merchandise, pose for selfies and shake hands.

It was a great trip and we earned a grand each (dollars that is) and came back home buoyant and ready for more gigs.

Chapter ten

We started booking gigs to play locally in and around London which then certainly brought us crashing down from our previous high. Apparently London is a fickle place when it comes to showing up to see a retro punk band play.

We played gigs all over town at various music venues in places like the Pipeline in Shoreditch, The Garage in Islington and the Fiddlers Elbow in Chalk Farm and many more but they were not attended anything like as well as our first two big gigs and we were disappointed to say the least. We had decent small crowds show up but it seemed far less excitable than when we played outside of our own manor.

Around this time Danny became disenchanted with the band and eventually we replaced him with Toby Thacker, another drummer mate of both Paul and Jonny's and who is, quite unbelievably, another phenomenal drummer.

So we stretched ourselves a bit and played over in Stockholm, Sweden.

This was The Ejected's first ever European gig.

Klub Anti-social was run by a group of Swedish girls who saved up their own hard earned Kroner to book and fly over Punk and Oi bands from around UK and Europe to play for them. These four girls were in it for the music and had a genuine love and interest in bringing over great bands to play for the punk rock fans of Stockholm. Apparently The Ejected are one of their very favourites and so they sounded over the moon when we agreed to do the gig. The fee they paid us was minimal but we didn't mind as they had agreed to pay for our return flights and booked us into a flash hotel in the centre of Stockholm for two nights. They also told us that our gig was sold out.

Stockholm was great and everyone was really friendly. The gig was in a basement bar that held 200 people. The two support bands (Nya Given and Les Frappes) had agreed to lend us their guitars, drums and amps to use so we didn't have to fly our gear over which we appreciated. After our sound check was finished in the hot, sweaty basement bar I went to cool off upstairs at a nearby bar for a few pints of the excellent Guinness they served there, as I was feeling a bit anxious with pre-gig nerves. I ended up staying in there chatting, smoking and drinking with the other punters until it was almost time to go and play the gig. The venue was packed out and they had managed to squeeze in over two hundred fans down there that were all excited to see us. That gig went great even though the stage was tiny and cramped, I could hardly move much as I had the drum kit up my arse and sound monitors right in front of me. The whole place was crammed and buzzing by the time we got started. It was fucking hot too. So fucking hot! We blistered our way through all the old

Ejected faves and stuck a few new ones in too. The crowd went crazy. Dancing, wrecking, moshing, cheering and singing along. Amazingly they seemed to know all the lyrics (sometimes better than me) and sang their hearts out. We did three encores and my throat was raw and parched when we were eventually allowed to come off stage and Jonny's fingers were bleeding and so were Toby's as we had played so fucking fast and hard.

I remember loving that trip and spending hours after the gig chatting to fans in the street with much needed cigarettes and several bottles of chilled water too. It was a great feeling. A memorable gig made possible by Tova, Louise, Jess and Heidi along with so many others. We went down very well and would definitely play out in Scandinavia again if we ever got asked.

Next was Scotland where they really do love their punk rock bands. We've headlined twice at Ivory Blacks in Glasgow and gone down great plus made some lovely friends for life up there too (Roddy, Kate, Dougie, Rowena, Anjie, Mandy, Joe, Wullie, Danny and Miriam). There are honestly more talented bands up there than I've ever seen anywhere down south. Rottweiler, The Zips, Fire Exit, Cuttin' Edge, Panik Attak and Half Charge to name drop but a few.

We also did a great support slot at The Fleece in Bristol with the UK Subs and again at Chinnery's, in Southend-On-Sea. So twice I have now been on the same bill as my punk rock faves and the legend that is Charlie Harper (that's if you don't include the Rebellion bills that we've shared the poster with them three times but played on different stages and days).

During this time we were still writing lots of new Ejected songs and really enjoying it, so I got on to my old mate Garry Bushell and asked him if he knew of any record companies that would be interested in possibly putting out a new Ejected album?

He said to try Diana Schuler at Randale Records over in Germany, as she had many of the old British punk bands signed up to her label. I had not heard of this label before but good old Gal furnished me with her email address and I sent her a message asking if she had heard of us or was interested at all?

Turns out she had and she was.

So we agreed terms and in 2016 we went into Perry Vale recording studio in Forest Hill, South London (very close to Lewisham, Catford and Grove Park near to where I had grown up as a kid yet again) and met Pat Collier the legendary producer and engineer of many famous acts over the years. He is coincidentally the chosen recording studio engineer of the UK Subs no less. So yet again I was in paradise.

We recorded thirteen new tracks in three days and called the new album 'Back From The Dead' and Diana at Randale Records let me do the sleeve artwork too and it was released shortly afterwards. Again I had that rare thrill of opening up the two boxes of new Ejected vinyl and CD's that got sent to us. Still as enthralled and excited about it after all these years.

We also made a promo video of 'Cops Are Coming' one of the more popular songs from that album. I'd never done a promo video before, not even back in the day. Imagine if we'd have made a video for 'Have You Got 10p?' who knows how much more it could have boosted that single up the charts or even gotten the band noticed a bit more maybe?

It was a weird experience for me having to pretend to sing along with the song being played back via a laptop. I had to mime (or lip sync as it's termed nowadays) and we had to do loads of retakes from different camera angles. It was a lot harder work than I ever expected it to be. A few days later Greg Taylor (one of Paul's tech mates) had edited it down to the final version which you can go and check out on YouTube or wherever. Greg did a great job too and it proved to be a very popular video amongst our loyal fan base.

Incidentally I did another promo video for an Ejected song called 'Alien Abduction' which was stop start animation cartoons drawn by me (obviously) to describe the lyrics. Paul sorted it out and it is also up on YouTube and came out really well.

Since reforming The Ejected we have written a total of 42 new songs on the three albums that were released on Randale Records. Not bad for an old timer I say, eh?

The other two albums that we recorded after 'Back From The Dead' are titled 'Game Of Survival' and 'Come 'N' Get It!'

Obviously the pandemic came along in 2020 and that brought all things to a halt and since then we have not played any gigs or recorded any new material.

During the lockdown periods I decided to concentrate on another passion of mine which is writing. All my life I have wanted to write a novel. Now suddenly I had both the time and inclination to give it a real go. In the past I had started many different novel ideas and written maybe forty or fifty pages of each storyline before either getting stuck or not having the time to concentrate on it what with work, the band or life in general getting in the way.

This time however, I had no excuses.

So I made myself write for between six to eight hours every day during lockdown and I eventually finished my first proper novel titled 'When I'm Dead And Gone'. Followed by, over the last two years more novels titled 'The Other Side Of Love', 'Where Nobody Knows My Name', 'Walk On The Wild Side', 'Born Under The Wrong Sign', 'With A Girl Like You', 'When The Sun Goes Down' and 'Ever Since You Went Away'.

All these titles I have self-published and have been uploaded to Amazon Kindle with Kat's kind help and I have another novel that is almost finished, ready and waiting to be uploaded, which is a medieval stroke fantasy novel called 'Quest For The Scared Chalice' which I wrote after Kat challenged me to see if I could stretch my writing talent to that particular genre.

All of my book titles have five word song titles too which I decided would be a sort of novelty gimmick if you like. And most of my novels (apart from the fantasy one) are thrillers set in Essex area and or in America and have contain down to earth characters, humour, music, danger, sex, thrills, romance, violence and intrigue so if you fancy reading any of them please go to Amazon Kindle where you can buy them as either a download (to your chosen electronic device) or in physical paperback form also.

I recently turned 64 which depressed the fuck out of me for a while but am still hopeful that The Ejected may still play some gigs in the future or that we might do another album too but we will have to wait and see.

I am very grateful for all the opportunities that I have been offered and have taken and have no real regrets (apart from not reforming the band a lot sooner or agreeing to record The Enemy Awaits ha, ha) about any of it.

Standing on that Florida stage and seeing so many fans enjoying all our songs filled me with pride and satisfaction.

When I finally do snuff it I will be leaving behind a body of work that will live on after I am dead and gone and that pleases me greatly as very few people in life get to fulfil their dreams. I also have the novels out there too which was another dream that I never thought would come true.

So there you have it the story of The Ejected and how it all happened.

If you do see me at a gig or standing outside a pub having a smoke then do come over and have a chat okay? Or of course if you really feel like it shout out "Oi Jim, have you got 10p?" and it'll make definitely make me smile. "Oi, Oi!"

DISCOGRAPHY

THE EJECTED EP'S

HAVE YOU GOT 10P? C/W CLASS OF 82 & ONE OF THE BOYS

NOISE FOR THE BOYS FAST & LOUD C/W I DON'T CARE & WHAT HAPPENED IN BRIGHTON?

PRESS THE BUTTON. RUSSIANS C/W 24 YEARS & IN THE CITY

THE EJECTED ALBUMS

A TOUCH OF CLASS

SPIRIT OF REBELLION

THE BEST OF THE EJECTED

BACK FROM THE DEAD

GAME OF SURVIVAL

COME 'N' GET IT

The Ejected with Pat Collier at Perry Vale Studios

Printed in Great Britain
by Amazon